ISBN-13: 978-1497594128

ISBN-10: 149759412X

This book is dedicated to my late friend and mentor
Len Burch

And

The volunteers on elected bodies

Who stand up against bullies, because of their moral duty and for what they believe is right, yet pay a price through ill health, the pain of injustice and/or humiliation. Nevertheless, they have the warmth that their integrity remains intact and are not alone being a member of the "ethical legion" of unsung heroes.

Vic Parks

April 2014

Co-ops and Mutuals:

Armageddon or Watershed?

and

Bullying and Control Freak Management

PREFACE

This book was initially written as a submission to the various enquiries into the Co-operative Group and Bank debacle. However, I decided to publish as I believe that it reaches far beyond the Co-operative and Mutual Sectors. Many volunteers and paid members of committees and boards - controlling trusts, charities, schools and colleges - may have similar problems. Staffs within the Public Sector, Industry and Commerce, who suffer from Control Freak Management, will have considerable empathy with the book's content. It has two major themes:

- analysing the problems of the Co-operative Group and proposals for its reform which can apply equally to other co-operatives and mutuals and
- The highly destructive phenomenon of Control Freak Management which uses bullying and fear to control people and make their lives a misery.

At the time of writing, the Co-operative Group [CG] is facing an economic meltdown and there is a real possibility of it going into liquidation. Until the collapse of the CG Bank, the organisation was a beacon of hope for idealistic Co-operators wishing to show that there is an alternative to greedy, unethical Corporate Capitalism. This marches around the world, seemingly unfettered and out of control. The divide between the rich and poor has become obscene. "The Market" pervades all parts of the Globe consuming everything in its path, destroying nations and communities, in the pursuit of profit and power for the few. The Murdock Empire is a case in point.

Nevertheless, the CG, although the largest retail co-operative in the UK, is a relatively small ship sitting in a sea of other Co-operatives and mutuals that are successful and viable. When many capitalist businesses go bankrupt little is heard. However, when a Co-operative or Mutual fails, there is media frenzy and opponents claim that social enterprise "does not work" compared with Corporate Capitalism.

Worker Co-ops
"Co-operation" is a diverse concept which embraces worker co-ops, Waitrose, John Lewis and many independent consumer co-ops. It would be utterly wrong to tar these organisations with the same brush as CG since many abide by the 19th Century "Founding Fathers" co-operative principles and values, **the bedrock of all co-operatives**. In my view, the worker co-ops are the heart and soul of the Co-operative Movement. For example, the very successful Suma workers co-operative (£35,000,000 turnover), still adheres to the principle of equal pay for all workers, from top to bottom. Operating in a world of Corporate Capitalism, which assumes the "conventional wisdom" of pay hierarchies being essential for a successful business, Suma exposes the lie.

The Mutual Sector
Within the mutual sector, Northern Rock (amongst others) failed, yet the Nationwide and smaller building societies still lead the way in financial success. Because Co-ops and Mutuals live in the "Market Philosophy" world, it is little wonder that they (and the people who control and run them) became influenced by the mainstream banks and their unethical practices.

Control Freak Management
The perception of "The Co-operative" by the public is that it is a "warm, caring, cuddly, honest and open organisation, built on ethics, owned by its members and run by "nice people" who adopt a "National Trust" ethos. **And so it should be!** However, this rosy façade hides a somewhat brutal regime in the **Co-operative Group (CG)** that is secretive, controlling, autocratic and vindictive.

Having witnessed it in my Further Education College, I am aware of the disastrous consequences of Control Freak Management - essentially, bullying, undermining and mentally destroying staff. I saw good lecturers distraught and in tears because of brutal bullying tactics. Several years after I left, the college went into Special Measures after failing Ofsted inspections. I fail to see how making staff live in fear and grossly unhappy in the workplace can be "productive," yet this scourge still continues today in the Public Sector, industry and commerce, the latter being where it originated. Perhaps it says a good deal about the psyche of the perpetrators who "torture" victims.

I believe that a major factor in the CG debacle, similar to the Enron scandal, is poor governance. **The servants (management) have become the masters.** Elected members primary role is to hold management to account, but they are little more than "nodding donkeys." It is widely known as the "Democratic Deficit." Members who ask "awkward" and persistent questions are ostracised, side lined or even ousted. There is a culture of "don't rock the boat" or: "You are with us or against us [the 'enemy']" which suppresses any sort of criticism of management or controlling cliques.

The CG hierarchical governance - Main Board, Regional Boards and Area Committees – contains controlling cliques and influential "quislings" who are "in bed" with Management and blindly support its decisions and policy. Many committee/board members just "go with the herd" for an easy life or out of fear. Some become "Co-operators" for the wrong reasons – a "wage," trips to four star hotels, and young, career politicians wishing to put "Co-op" on their CVs. [Perhaps not now with the negative publicity!].

To some extent, this book is a "case study" of institutional bullying, which can happen in many organisations. Staffs have trade unions, legal support and appeals tribunals. However, volunteers have none and are vulnerable. When victimised, they are on their own. **This book offers a proposal to protect them through legislation**.

I have offered samples of my articles to illustrate that many of the issues identified by this book, were raised consistently over many years. Although I have had legal advice that the book is "Fair Comment" with unlikely grounds for Court action, the References Section is a safeguard. It is the documented evidence to substantiate the claims against named individuals. Most bullies are vindictive and some may well attempt to censor this book by threatening the author. These documents are essential for this work. The book is published in the Public Interest and in good faith.

The various enquiries into the Co-operative Group will report soon. They are likely to focus upon institutional failings, poor governance, Main Board incompetence and so on. To some extent, they may well be looking for "scape goats" [e.g. CEO Marks?] but, as Myners commented, all elected members are responsible right down to the lowest tiers in the Democratic Structure (Area Committees). Myners, in particular, will offer proposals for re-designing the democratic structure. However, no matter how good the structure, it is likely to be filled by the same old faces and cronies. The destructive Control Freak culture will continue unless this fundamental issue is addressed. So much depends upon the quality, ethics, attitudes and integrity of those within the organisation. Caring, just, decent and dedicated Co-operators are needed in a Co-operative; but how can the system percolate them to the top and into positions of power?

Will this Co-operative Movement crisis be Armageddon or a Watershed? Failure of CG is deeply damaging to the argument that Social Enterprise is a viable alternative to the greed of Corporate Capitalism. If the CG reforms to become a truly democratic, warm, caring, cuddly, honest and open organisation, built on ethics, owned by its members and run by "nice people" who adopt a "National Trust" ethos, it will be a watershed in the Co-operative historical annals.

Vic Parks   April 2014

© **Vic Parks 2014**

CONTENTS

INTRODUCTION

1. One of the **AIMS** of this book is to help the Co-operative Group become a truly **"Sharing and Caring Co-op,"** helping it to return to its Principles and Values. This not just a personal aim but one shared by many grassroots co-operators who have, for example, written into the Co-operative News for many years. Another key aim is to give **protection to elected members,** who are somewhat defenceless, vulnerable and at the mercy of the Secretariat and controlling cliques, **through legislation.** To this end, to give them the same rights enjoyed by employees. The key proposals are in the "Overview" **(para. 37, 55 & 468).**

2. When I first decided to document what happened to me, I did not realise that it was going to be a substantial literary work. I had thought it would be a relatively simple statement. However, I am dealing with quite unpleasant people who might seek revenge because I am speaking out. For example, threatening to sue for Defamation, Libel, etc. Thus, I have taken great care to ensure my allegations can be supported by documentation. It appears to be a trait of Control Freak, Autocratic Management to be vengeful and vindictive. Having spent many years in Civil Courts as a LIP, including the Court of Appeal (no mean feat for a LIP), I have acquired a rudimentary knowledge of Law. However, I am disadvantaged as I do not have a lawyer advising me.

3. It has been a painful experience raking up what befell me at the hands of those who set out to harass, victimise and bully me. Being in senior positions, they abused their power. Although I put on a "brave face," it was extremely unpleasant lasting much of my time serving the Co-operative Group as a voluntary, elected member on an Area Committee (one time Chair). People (usually staff), working under Control Freak Management cultures, are constantly looking over their shoulders and living in fear, especially those employed and dependent upon a livelihood. Many politicians may empathise with this but acquire a "thick Skin" and/or comfort themselves with clear consciences, with their integrity intact.

4. The "Long Distance Innovators" and historical characters who challenge the status quo invariably suffer abuse for their beliefs. *"You can be the most likeable, decent person in the world but someone will hate you for these qualities!"* - Jesus, Socrates being early historical victims. Fortunately, it is a privilege to live in a society where we are not tortured and shot for our "off message, radical views or not going with the herd"! However, there are other sanctions ruling cliques can employ in contemporary society: bullying, side-lining, vilification, ostracization, undermining and so on.

5. As a volunteer, I could have walked away at any time, which close friends often urged. However, if one is passionate about a cause, there is more to life than the pursuit of personal happiness. Added to that, I survived because my integrity was intact and most of the "nice" people I know in politics and the Co-operative Movement seemed to respect, like and support me. As one former Area Committee member commented recently: "You fought for us!" Some years ago, a retired Regional Secretary said: "Keep the faith," when he could see I was under attack from the hierarchy for speaking out.

6. Although the book may appear somewhat voluminous, there are "short cuts." The **"OVERVIEW"** sub-titled "The Roots of the Co-operate Group Disaster" and the section headed **"BULLYING"** (based upon the FSA letter 2008) are essential for the Treasury Select Committee. Sections on **CONFIDENTIALITY, DEMOCRACY AND FREE SPEECH** impinge upon the bullying section, but perhaps more important for the other on-going enquiries, particularly "Governance" (e.g. Kelly, Mynors). The **APPENDIX** entitled: **"In Defence of Integrity"** is a detailed rebuttal of the (then) Regional Secretary's (Karen Froggatt's) allegations presented to the Regional Board behind my back. These were, in my view, concocted to provide "grounds" (excuses) to "discipline"

me so that I could be silenced or ousted. Although it may give some insight into how management tries to get targeted people out of an organisation, it may not be essential reading. Equally, the **REFERENCES** section contains documentation supporting my allegations of institutional bullying, etc. For example, the SE Regional Board's decisions were made and minuted behind my back - procedures which went against "Natural Justice" and the Co-op principle of "No personal attacks."

7. **CONFIDENTIALITY** is contained within the CG Code of Conduct which the Secretariat can use to control and silence outspoken elected members. Because the Secretariat defines what is confidential it can manipulate "evidence" against those with their "heads above the parapet" ("trouble makers, who ask questions"). It can control information and thus operate a form of censorship. This section is sub-headed: "The Code of Conduct - A Noose to Hang Dissidents?" It is based on a paper/article I wrote in 2008 analysing the CG Code of Conduct. For lay elected members, the Code is a minefield as it is quite subjective and can be interpreted in various ways. Thus, it easy for the Secretariat to pick off (in their eyes) "the awkward squad." Elected members need to be lawyers to avoid pitfalls. Taken literally, no one can speak to anyone outside of their committee/Board, **which has serious consequences for Governance.** For example, it is important (for training purposes) that members from different committees in a region and nationally, can share experience, knowledge and best practice. I understand that, recently, the Code was being used to discipline an elected member. Thus, little has changed, since my involvement with CG.

8. **FREE SPEECH** is essential for democracy and democracy is at the heart of a Co-operative or Mutual. Although the Secretariat hypocritically espouses Co-operative Principles, there is little doubt that it tries to stifle free speech. It wishes to control what goes into the Public Domain, as "it knows best" and to "protect management." We live in an age of "spin" where an articulate representative ("The Voice") of an organisation (e.g. a utility) tries to convince the public that "everything is fine," even when the evidence is to the contrary. Although the Secretariat may believe that it is right to defend the CG, taken to extremities, it stifles debate and deters elected representatives holding management to account, their fundamental role and duty. There needs to be a balance of co-operative principles of honesty and openness with breaching confidentiality that may, for example, assist a competitor. Several articles are included in this section, which I had published on this reoccurring theme. My analysis of the CG Code of Conduct is based upon documents circulated at the time. I guess little has been revised and, if it has, it will be a further "tightening of the noose."

9. **DEMOCRACY** allegedly makes co-operatives and mutuals different from PLCs. Theoretically; the "business" is "owned and controlled by its members." Janet Cato pointed out that problems arise when Co-ops become too big (Society for Co-operative Studies Conference 2010) – i.e. "small is beautiful." In small organisations, such as worker co-ops, it is relatively easy to communicate with all the members and involve them directly in decision making. However, with the representative democratic model, as in the CG **(see para 260 - 268),** the major criticism of many activists is that the hierarchy becomes remote from the grassroots membership. Thus, the Main and Regional Boards made decisions of which, probably, the majority of the membership disapproved.

10. At the time of the last Constitutional Review, Dame Pauline Green (then CEO of Co-operatives UK) argued in an article (Co-op News 22 Jan 2008) that there should be some form of One Member One Vote (OMOV), especially for Main/Regional Directors. This is little different from Building societies. On-line voting, etc. facilitates easy and economic voting. However, as Pauline pointed out: *"(will the Review) be a co-operative fudge put together to defend vested interests and appease local sentiment?"* This proved to be the case. In a draft article with the working title of "Constitutional Review – Self Interest Rules OK?" I also predicted the Review's outcome: it changed little in terms of Governance.

11. If the current (cynically) (UN)democratic representation decides the future structures post Kelly, Myners, Treasury Select Committee, history will repeat itself. **Out of self-interest, little will change, other than a little bit of "cherry picking," as the current elected members are unlikely to reform themselves. "Consultation" with members is a sham, a CON and inSULT to the nATION**! As I stated in an "article" after the Constitutional Review in 2007/8: *"At the time of the Constitutional Review, I predicted that it would change little other than perhaps the discriminatory Age Rule and tinker with some structures. This appears to be the case. With the "Top Table" firmly in control of the process, it was to be expected…[consultation with the membership] is often a fixed agenda with the outcomes largely predetermined…What I witnessed at the ["consultation"] roadshow was the usual sham…It is a sterile, controlled exercise…to legitimatise their ["Top Table"/Management's] decisions …in private without scrutiny, transparency or explanation."* Co-op News, 10 June 2008 **(Please read full "article" Ref 16).**

12. Lord Myners in a Co-op News interview stated: "It will then be for the Board to decide whether to accept my recommendations in total or in part and whether it wishes to put any of those recommendations to the AGM. I don't have any power to put anything to the AGM…" This is somewhat depressing and the various enquiries could be a complete waste of time. Grassroots hopes will be raised, but then dashed. However, if the Review/Enquiry was to consider legislation to create a framework for large co-operatives, there is more chance of a truly democratic structure representative of the views and aspirations of the ordinary members. There are many "Co-operative academics" that could produce a considered and objective structure, perhaps under the wings of Co-operatives UK and the International Co-operative Alliance. Instead of the "usual suspects" with self-interest voting on new Governance proposals, perhaps they should be voted for on-line or through regional meetings with duplicated documentation and agendas.

13. In my "Overview, I suggest that all those in the elected bodies are responsible with regard to the collapse of the CG and, indirectly, the Co-op Bank. Although a bold step, perhaps they, individually, should be replaced unless they can show evidence of standing up to the cronyism and Secretariat. Clearly, some good people would go. On an interim basis, respected, co-operative experienced members could fill the current structures (perhaps retirees).

OVERVIEW

The Roots of the Co-operative Group Disaster

14. *Note that this section ONLY applies to Co-operative Group, since "Co-operation" is a diverse concept which embraces worker co-ops, Waitrose, John Lewis and many other, smaller independent consumer co-ops. It would be utterly wrong to tar these organisations with the same brush as CG since many abide by the "Founding Fathers" co-operative principles and values, **the bedrock of all co-operatives**. In my view, the worker co-ops are the heart and soul of the Co-operative Movement. For example, the very successful Suma workers co-operative (£35,000,000 turnover), which still adheres to the principle of workers equal pay from top to bottom despite operating in a world of Corporate Capitalism holding the "conventional wisdom" of pay hierarchies being essential for a successful business.*

15. The perception of "The Co-operative" by the public is that it is a "warm, caring, cuddly, honest and open organisation, built on ethics, owned by its members and run by "nice people" who adopt a "National Trust" ethos. **And so it should be!** However, this rosy façade hides a somewhat brutal regime in the **Co-operative Group (CG)** that is secretive, controlling, autocratic and vindictive.

16. "Old timer co-operators," say that there was always tension between CG management and elected representatives. However, in recent decades this, in my view, has become exacerbated with the rise of a "Control Freak Management" culture that will not tolerate criticism and will try to silence outspoken, questioning members. As "Management knows best," it prevents elected members from "doing things," unless they are benign and will not interfere with the Management's agenda.

17. I left the CG as an elected representative (Former Chair of an Area Committee) some years ago, but I foretold, in my many Co-operative Articles, the disaster that has befallen CG. The worst thing about this affair is that the many dedicated co-operators, of which I am one, try to promote Mutualism and Co-operatives as a plausible alternative to Global Capitalism and the Free Market Economy. The CG failure has totally undermined our position. From my contacts within the CG, the Main/Regional Boards are running around like headless chickens, trying to hold back the tsunami which has already engulfed them.

18. Similar to the Enron scandal, a major problem is governance. **The servants (management) have become the masters.** Elected members are little more than "nodding donkeys." It is widely known as the "democratic deficit." Members who asked questions (their role!) are ostracised, side lined or even ousted. There is a culture of "don't rock the boat" or: "you are with us or against us [the 'enemy']" which suppresses criticism of management or controlling cliques. The CG hierarchical structure of governance - Main Board, Regional Boards and Area Committees – contains controlling cliques and influential "quislings" who are "in bed" with Management, supporting its decisions and policy. Many committee/board members just "go with the herd" for an easy life or out of fear. Some are often in it for the wrong reasons – a "wage," trips to four star hotels, and so on. The latest phenomenon is young, career politicians wanting to put "Co-op" on their CVs. [perhaps not now!].

19. Although many "Co-operators" espouse Co-operative principles and values, they do not live by them. At the time of the merger in 2008, elected members were offered "compensation" if they stood down. One such person was a Director on the Bank Board, Main Board, Regional Board and Area Committee. Unlike a Main Board director who took compensation and left all his elected positions, she retained her position on the Area Committee but took compensation which totalled

some £75,000. Although within the rules (set by the Main Board), it was somewhat immoral. Thus, she kept some of her sphere of influence, yet had a substantial sum of money.

20. The "Do not rock the boat" attitude leads to cover-ups. One such incident happened when it was discovered that, after the death of a Co-operative Party Branch Chair, he had stolen some £3000. I, in a minority of one, wanted to try and claim back the money from his estate. However, other members of the committee refused and wanted to hush it up. Although not part of the CG, most members were past or present Area Committee members.

21. Over the years, CG Senior Management has destroyed or, at least, undermined the democratic control (if there ever was any). Instead of supporting elected members [its role] it seeks to control or intimidate them. Because of the Control Freak ethos, elected members, even at Main Board level, are bullied or just keep quiet. Although I appreciate the pressure they are under, they are somewhat cowardly.

22. "Quislings" not only blindly follow management agendas but, if in positions of power, will meter out "punishment" to "dissident" elected members. I, for example, was publicly attacked for my views, publications or questions by the current SE Regional Board Chair and her predecessor. The intention is to belittle "culprits" and emotionally crush them. I stood up to management as Area Committee Chair and was victimised. My crime was to ask questions and to get published in the main organ of Co-operative information, the Co-operative News. Perhaps I was seen as too influential and a threat. The SE Regional Board "ordered" my Area Committee not to appoint me as a delegate.

23. **Bullying is endemic in CG.** Research showed that18% of staff reported bullying **(Ref 4 & para 25).** Potentially, this could be 20,000 people. In my college I witnessed the disastrous consequences of Control Freak Management - essentially, bullying, undermining and mentally destroying staff. I saw good lecturers distraught and in tears because of brutal bullying tactics. Several years after I left, the college went into Special Measures after failing Ofsted inspections. I fail to see how making staff live in fear and grossly unhappy in work can be "productive," yet this scourge still continues today in the Public Sector, industry and commerce, the latter being where it originated. Evidence of bullying was from a senior co-operators at that time:

24. *It is however a sad day when a professional officer chooses to break with a 134 year old convention that paid officials do not engage in a personal attack on democratically elected lay directors.....* *(the) Movement is already over-dominated by paid officers.... Employees of the Movement – who will not rest until the voice of the lay member has been completely silenced." Alan Middleton, a lecturer and senior director, 23 Aug 2005*

25. *"...in a number of societies there have been instances of bullying behaviour, defamation, vindictiveness or their unwillingness to accept collective responsibility. The result can be that some colleagues might fear to participate at all. Maybe these situations contribute to the cases where directors do not contribute to meetings for fear of being bullied, intimidated or embarrassed.....for them to occur in a co-operative is shameful We shall see whether the Code of Conduct is able to help stamp any existing behaviour out." Geraint Day, Director and Co-op Party NEC member, 28 June 2005*

26. In an article just before the merger between CG and United Co-operative headed: "United Should Look before They Leap," **(Ref 1, p2)** I foretold all. I was deeply concerned because the merger would mean CG controlling 85% of UK food retail co-operatives. It put too much power into the hands of just a few people who could, indirectly, control organisations I mentioned in another article

"Group's Cuts are Damaging the Fabric of the [Co-op] Movement," 9-23 Aug 2005 **(Ref 1, p1).** I was concerned about cuts to the various co-operative organisations it helps fund: Woodcraft Folk, Guilds, Co-operative UK, Co-operative Press, Co-op Party, Co-operative Education, etc. This included elected representatives' development and conferences which are essential for them to understand their role and issues affecting them.

27. The Project Exchequer article provoked a great deal of support with follow up letters. The following letter extracts from concerned, senior co-operators, printed in the Co-operative News (prior to merger), reinforce the deep concerns I have:

28. *"...many Area Committee members are incensed at the perceived cynicism of the (Main) Board in deferring the Quinquennial Review, only to introduce shortly afterwards and without any prior consultation, Project Exchequer, a management led project that purports to make savings but which in reality are cuts; a project that takes no account of the Co-operative Difference; and a project that is more concerned with implementing decisions already taken by the Group Board rather than involving members in reaching and taking ownership of those decisions." Ron Hunter, former Regional Secretary, 23 Aug 2005*

29. ***"Vic Parks is absolutely right in his recent article headlined Group cuts are damaging he fabric of our Movement.*** *My only criticism is that he appears to seriously underestimate the threat..... I feel that our democratic birth right and institutions are once again under attack – only this time from within.... The present regional board system is anti-democratic and simply does not work....Let the Co-operative Group hierarchy have their excessive pay and pension if you must, but don't let them steal your co-operative democracy." Philip Rapier Regional Committee member, 23 Aug 2005*

30. I believe this was the final straw and the Secretariat decided to try and silence me. I underwent a relentless attack from the Secretariat. Initially, this came from Karen Froggett the [then] Regional Secretary who was backed her managers - seniors in the membership hierarchy, the Company Secretary [Nick Eyre] and his deputy [Moira Lees] – resulting in some thirty letters. For whatever reasons, the former (who was pushed out on "Gardening Leave") was replaced by the latter. It was alleged that the article was in breach of confidentiality. When I questioned which part of the article breached confidentiality, they could only point to the mention of Euro Co-op which was going to get a cut in funding and had not been told. Of course, that was based entirely on their word and it was not substantiated. In my view, it was a frivolous point, used as a spurious excuse to attack me. The Co-op News editor who published the article had said that the cuts were in the Public domain **(See Bullying section, para 56 for detailed account).**

31. I understand that the Secretariat was furious about my article. Probably, this was because of its hatred of criticism, challenge to its "authority," and its obsession with secrecy and control. Confidentiality is used as a weapon to control lay members. One such member, the late Reverend Hugh Bridge was suspended from his Area Committee for three months. He was accused of disclosing information [whistleblowing?] about selling off Co-op departmental stores. This was a highly contentious decision by the Main Board at the time. I often wonder whether the pressure they put on him contributed to his death by heart attack, some short time later.

32. Since the attack on me by the Senior Secretariat basically failed, the then Regional Secretary (Karen Froggett) tried another tack. She produced and circulated a spurious and defamatory document, which alleged so-called "misconduct" **(see Appendix para 331 - 445).** The "evidence" was somewhat trivial and was provided by two other employees of the Secretariat, one of which (the then Area committee Secretary) had often showed a personal dislike for me and was very difficult to deal with. As I understand it, she had altercations with other Area Committees.

33. The document was presented to the Regional Board **behind my back, without an opportunity to defend myself.** The Board used this as an excuse to pass a motion condemning me **(Ref. 9 p 1)**. This is hardly surprising since the Chair seemed to dislike me as she had previously attacked me publicly and in print **(Ref 12).** She also appeared to be an ally of the Regional Secretary. In politics and Public Service, it is very easy to acquire "enemies" and I am sure I had many on Regional Board. Perhaps this was because I was prepared to "rock the boat" by being outspoken, asking "awkward" questions, personality differences or perhaps jealousy/resentment by having a high profile through my many published letters and articles in the Co-operative Press.

34. Although I was elected Chair, by my Area Committee, to make a stand against Management, it forced me to stand down. Later, I was told that if they had not "disciplined" me the Regional Board had threatened to suspend the Area Committee. In an unprecedented move (and probably against the rules), the Regional Board's Vice-chair attended the "disciplinary" meeting. He was a manager and an overbearing man who stated at the outset: "I want this decided now!" Acting as a sort of "Gauleiter," he was there to pressurise my committee. Prior the meeting, I had circulated to my committee, a document entitled "In Defence of Integrity and Character" **(See Appendix para 331 - 449)**, in which I tried to defend myself against Karen Froggett's allegations. I understand that three of the committee fought for me, but the rest just went along with the Regional Board pressure.

35. As there is not an independent appeal process, I wrote a detailed complaint to the FSA. However, I understand that the FSA has no power regarding the governance of Co-operatives. In a conversation with an FSA official it was said that I could take the Group to Court. But what chance would a lay person have against a [then] £9 Billion company with unlimited legal and financial resources, fighting the Secretariat which had no personal financial risk? One deceased member, who took on the Group, had to pay legal costs out of his estate.

36. In similar circumstances, employees have trade union support. Indeed, I understand that senior Group officers reached out-of-Court settlements in recent times. In my view, it is indicative of a Control Freak Management culture when employees have to resort to tribunals and courts. Employees have protection from Employment Law, legal advice and support. **Lay representatives do not and are, fundamentally, on their own.** When so identified as "marked trouble-makers," ones friends and supporters disappear. Others fear being seen to be in association with "dissident voices" in case they are also ostracised. One employee said to me "I should not be seen talking to you." In another incident, when talking to an MP's advisor, a prominent CG member of staff and NEC Co-op Party member, sidled up and said: "you shouldn't talk to him. He's dangerous."

37. For me and others who faced similar problems [in particular bullying, side lining or victimisation], **there needs to be legislation for an independent appeals service, perhaps an Ombudsman, protection under Employment Law, the same rights as employees and legal representation paid by the Co-operative/Mutual and automatic membership of a trade union or employee association. Further, to change a culture of bullying, oppressive, autocratic managers and seniors in organisations who are the perpetrators need to be given training/counselling to change their behaviour. If they persist, they should face disciplinary procedures and, ultimately, removal. The message needs to be unequivocal: bullying in all its various forms will not be tolerated.**

38. Bullying problems go far beyond the Co-operative/Mutual sector and exists in many voluntary organisations, industry, commerce and political parties, NHS Trusts, school governors, trustees, etc. When employees take employers to tribunals, and win, the outcome is usually compensation but no reinstatement. Added to that, they may well find future employment difficult, even though a totally

innocent victim of perhaps a sadistic, vicious senior. There are many cases of sexual harassment where the target of a manager, who refuses to engage in sexual activity with him/her, is unjustly accused with invented allegations. In Education, lecturers can harass students by making their marks go up or down depending upon whether their students comply with or refuse their sexual advances.

39.   The injustice of a bullying culture is that the perpetrators often go unpunished. Indeed, some are promoted within the organisation! If we believe in a caring society (core Co-operative principle), bullying, victimisation and the misuse of power needs to be eradicated. In my view, employees, elected representatives, etc. are more productive when happy rather than when working in a climate of fear. This has wider implications for society in general.

40.   For most of my time in CG, I tried to campaign for greater democracy, free speech, caring management and greater co-operation between management and elected representatives (especially within my published and unpublished articles/documents). I could see where CG's oppressive culture would lead and this is a major reason why CG is in a mess and on the brink of collapse. Added to this, the controversy surrounding Flowers (ex-Chair of Co-op Bank) and the appointment of Marks as CEO, just before I left, are deeply damaging to the Co-operative ideals. Was Marks's expansionist agenda - buying up Somerfield and other chains - too much, too fast and just feeding his ego? The Britannia Building Society was the reckless acquisition mortally wounding the Co-op Bank. Where was the "due diligence," especially in view of the home loans scandals in 2008? Were the CG's auditors [KPMG] at fault?

41.   Allegedly, Marks bullied and berated members of the Main Board who opposed him. I sympathise with them. One ex-Board member said to me recently: "I just got fed up with banging my head against a brick wall." However, did the quislings and gutless "yes people" on the Regional and Main Boards fail to do their duty? The Co-operative Bank was the money making arm of Group. Now that has gone, it has serious implications for the Food Retail, which struggles against the power of the Big Four supermarkets.

42.   **REFORM OF THE CO-OPERATIVE GROUP**

43.   The appointment of Ursula Lidbetter may be a step in the right direction. She comes from Lincoln Co-op whose president is Alan Middleton - a genuine, decent co-operator - and Ursula receives similar accolades. However, although she may well have zeal and genuine ambitions to bring about root and branch reform, the "usual suspects," cliques and cronies will not want to reform themselves. Many of them are still in the same positions of power, when I left, some five years ago, and are likely to resist change. Over the years, various "reviews" changed little, even though many grassroots members wanted greater democracy and wider decision making, to overcome the "democratic deficit." In my view, **there needs to be legislation guided by the "good, nice guys/gals"** – not the power seeking control freaks who act out of self-interest – to build a co-operative model adaptable to suit individual circumstances.

44.   A co-operative principle is that it is owned and run by its members. It is a paradox that shareholders in PLCs have more rights than co-operative members. They can attend PLC AGMs, yet the CG elected representative model and delegate system to CG AGM means relatively few people can make decisions. Delegations are also easy to control by the Secretariat and its quislings. Perhaps the regular use of referendums gives ordinary members greater control and meets the Co-operative principle of one member one vote. When I was Chair, it was my philosophy to be the "servant of the committee," not its dictator.

45. Many outside the Co-operative Movement view it with "rose tinted glasses" – warm, caring and "cuddly." Perhaps it was so in days gone past but the "Market philosophy," individualism, consumerism, autocratic management styles, etc. has greatly influenced its ethos in the last few decades. By stating that CG has a Control Freak management style, it has to be said that I have met many staff in the Membership team who are pleasant, decent Co-operators with good, Co-operative values. Invariably, the ethos of any organisation is set and implemented by senior members of the organisation.

46. I know many decent, genuine co-operators of integrity but they either "keep their heads down" or leave their elected positions. For a co-operative to function properly, it needs to be firmly grounded in its ethical principles. Co-operation is more than just a "business." It is a set of principles and values to act as a beacon for future generations living in a world where there is potential for enormous social upheaval, unrest and anarchy. Unfortunately, CG has lost its way by, for example, appointing managers and other staff who are not true co-operators. We have seen the rise of "Corporate Co-operation," the adoption of the "Big Business mentality" which is greatly influenced by the "Market philosophy" rather than Co-operative principles and values, the bedrock of all Co-operative and Mutual organisations.

47. True Co-operation is an alternative to autocratic, totalitarian states. As argued above, **to be effective, the right of free speech and criticism needs to be rigorously upheld with lay representatives properly supported, protected and free from fear of speaking out.** Fear felt by "whistle blowers" and management cover-ups are reasons for the mid Staffordshire, Colchester and Cumbrian hospitals' scandals.

48. Being inheritors of the Co-operative vision, the current elected members are the "Guardians" with an obligation to uphold what the founders fought for and established. To prevent bullying, side lining, harassment or victimisation, legislation is needed **(see para 37 & 55).**

49. The Co-op News 19 June 2012 headline was: "Bank Named Best in Europe." In just 12 months it is one of the "worst." Why? Is it incompetence? In my view the whole of the elected reps need to be replaced. Short term, this might need quick, short legislation. Some good, genuine people will go. Perhaps some sort of interim board.... made up of perhaps past co-operators who are genuine and untarnished or those existing elected members who have put their heads over the parapet in the past and stood up to the CG autocratic management. But who chooses them?

50. A Co-operative principle is the one of "caring for others." **This Control Freak ethos needs to be eradicated to create a caring, open, honest, democratic organisation** run by true co-operators who are more interested in the "greater good" of ordinary members, than that of self-interest and power. Discussion and the expression of views need to be done without fear of retribution. Unfortunately, there are many politicos in positions of power who know how to use systems, "shaft people" and "climb the greasy pole." Ex-Chair Flowers is an example of this. If they cannot be ousted, they need to be neutralised to protect genuine co-operators, perhaps again by legislation. Nevertheless, from my experience, not all politicians are the same as I have met many decent, genuine people in politics. Unfortunately, the "nasty ones" often side-line them or force them out.

51. In this Overview, I have made various allegations, particularly bullying, cronyism and "Control Freakery." A "symptom" of this is a high turnover in staff and cases of Grievance brought against managers by employees, usually supported by Trade Unions. Members of the Select Committee and the current enquiries [e.g. by Kelly] into the Co-op, need to contact former employees and elected representatives to encourage them to come forward. They may need to be released from CG imposed gagging clauses. I know of several cases where staff had to take out Grievance procedures and go to

tribunals, and there are probably many more. Even if settled before formal proceedings (as often happens), they are still indicative of the worst sort of management: autocratic, Control Freak, bullying. Hopefully, former Board members and elected representatives, who have had similar problems to me and others, will share their experience. However, some may not due to the psychological pain (Depression) raking up the past and probable injustice, fear or not wishing to damage the Co-op Group further. There is also a view that co-operators should focus upon the positives. For example, a co-operative "discussion" site said:

52. *"On this site highly critical texts received about the bank's management will not be published, as the issue is being investigated at more than one level and most co-operators will prefer to emphasise positive developments."*

53. This form of self-censorship avoids the in-depth discussion and analysis that the Co-operative Group situation needs to get to the root causes of its collapse. It implicitly enables the perpetuation of the Control Freak and bullying culture to continue. If some of my proposals are adopted, the Co-operative Group may move back towards a culture of care and emerge a stronger organisation genuinely embedded in its principles and values. However, many with vested interests will not want reform.

54. About five years ago, I had a high level meeting with Treasury officials at the time of the Review into Co-operative and Credit Union legislation. Many of the ideas I forward above were presented to them. I believe that the senior officials were interested but not put them into legislation. Perhaps the Co-op Bank would not have collapsed and CG may not be on its knees if they had been taken up. Although the horse may have bolted, better late than never to help future members or others in non-CG co-operative and mutual organisations!

55. In summary, the following needs to be set in legislation, where appropriate:

   a) an independent regulatory body for members to complain to (e.g. FSA);
   b) an independent Appeals Tribunal (similar to those for employees);
   c) a statutory right for elected lay members to belong to a trade union (or its equivalent) to give independent support. The membership fees to be paid for by the co-operative they represent;
   d) full whistle blowing rights, similar to those afforded to staff;
   e) to stop the Secretariat using confidentiality as a means to unjustifiably gag members, a set of guidelines on confidentiality and an independent committee to adjudge what should be kept confidential is needed.
   f) Retraining/counselling of perpetrators in the bullying culture, or sanctions against them. Ultimately, their removal.

BULLYING AND VICTIMISATION

A Control Freak Culture?

56   When I look back over my files, I am clear in my mind that I was subject to institutional bullying and victimisation. It went from the top of the Co-operative Group (CG) organisation to the lower tiers of Management. This consisted of the Company Secretary (Nick Eyre), his deputy (Moira Lees, later to replace him), the SE Regional Secretary (Karen Froggett, now a senior manager in the Membership Department) and the SE Area Committee Secretary (Collette Harber). Although Management led, the so-called democratic structure in the guise of the Regional Board also took part in the bullying. The main protagonist was the Chair (Adrienne Lowe, who is still Chair), but the Regional Board members at the time, were equally culpable, by association, when it passed motions naming me. As I stated in my substantive document, many sit on committees and Boards, yet say nothing. This is probably out of fear, in case **they** would be ostracised in the same way if they were to defend me.

57   It has been a painful and somewhat depressing experience raking up, yet again, what I suffered and the injustice of it all. My "crime" was a fundamental belief in Co-operative principles and values: honesty, openness, democracy – free speech, asking questions **and holding management to account, which is the fundamental duty of elected members** – and caring for others. Had it not been for the collapse of the CG, I would have just let it go and tried to get on with other things I had neglected in my life. This I have done since I left around 2008. However, this is an opportunity to change the CG's culture for the benefit and protection of future elected members. As stated in the Overview (The Roots of the CG Disaster), this goes far beyond CG and applies to elected members on boards and committees who act in a voluntary capacity (e.g. School/hospital trust governors, members of committees, trustees).

58   The institutional victimisation and bullying was largely management led. The documentation clearly identifies Karen Froggett (the then Regional Secretary) as the main protagonist who was supported by members of the Regional Board. I find it very hard to understand how a relatively intelligent body of people failed to ask the question: "What is Vic's view on Karen Froggett's allegations?" Yet, it seems that they took her allegations as being totally true, ignoring any notions of "natural justice." Thus, it appears to have acted as a "Kangaroo Court" by passing motions that they knew would be circulated around the various Area Committees (see Regional Board Minutes Dec 2005) and probably beyond. I am sure that there would also be rumour mongers blackening my name and reputation. A usage, for example, was when the RB motions were reiterated in a letter to me by Nick Eyre (Company Secretary) **(Ref 9, p 1)**.

59   It provides an example of how complicit the Senior Management was in this affair as **he (and his deputy, Moira Lees) was legally trained and ought to have appreciated that "natural justice" ("a duty to act fairly") had not been done.** At the very least, I had not been entitled to a defence. This is why I advocate legal protection for elected members **(see "Roots of the Co-operative Disaster" paras 37 & 55 & 468)**. It is utterly wrong for them to be defenceless when facing institutional bullying and victimisation. As I said in the FSA letter **(para 140)** I was hung on a metaphorical gibbet for all to see, as a warning to others not to speak out or "rock the boat."

60   The documented evidence of the institutional bullying lies in the letter to the FSA dated May 2007, but this has been expanded to aid more in-depth discussion and to cover further instances of

intimidation and bullying. It is ironical that a CG document "Respect Works" (circulated Mar 2007) from Human Resources states:

61   *Everyone Within the Group has a responsibility to treat each other with respect. It is how we would wish to be treated ourselves, it creates a productive working environment and it fits strongly with the values of the Society.*

62   *The Co-operative Group is fully committed to removing bullying, harassment or discrimination in any form from-the organisation.*

63   **Although aimed at staff, why should not the same principles equally apply to elected members? Or is it simply that the Senior Secretariat ignored its own policies? Irrespective of the legality, surely there was a moral duty of care? From the next extracts it is plain that the way I was treated fits the policy's bullying, harassment and discrimination criteria:**

64   *What bullying, harassment and discrimination means: Bullying may be characterised as either persistent or a serious (one-off) incident deemed to involve offensive, intimidating, malicious or insulting behaviour, Additionally, bullying may be an abuse or misuse of power through means that undermine, humiliate, denigrate or injure the recipient.* **In the FSA letter, (para 140) I raised the issue of Karen Froggatt and Adrienne Lowe misusing their power.**

65   *Harassment, in general terms, is unwanted and unreasonable conduct' affecting the dignity of men and women in the workplace or any other work related environment or situation.* **[There is little doubt in my mind that my dignity had been harmed and that I was intentionally humiliated].**

66   *This policy applies whether the incident(s) involves an employee (either temporary or permanent), supplier or contractor on all of the Co-operative Group premises, at work-related or organised event or at any time and place where the Society is being represented by the individual.* **[Clearly, this would apply to elected members and there was some argument that, for administrative purposes, they were treated to be staff.]**

67   *The Respect Works Policy has been put in place to reinforce the Society's commitment to eradicating bullying and harassment, define key, inappropriate behaviours and highlight the avenues of support available, including the Society's existing Grievance and Disciplinary procedures.* **[It would appear that the Secretariat assumed that this did not apply to elected members, although I argued in "Roots of the Co-operative Disaster" (para 37) that protection through legislation is needed]. ACAS'S definition further reinforces CG policy and, perhaps, goes beyond:**

68   *Bullying and harassment means any unwanted behaviour that makes someone feel intimidated, degraded, humiliated or offended. It is not necessarily always obvious or apparent to others, and may happen in the workplace without an employer's awareness.*

69   *Bullying or harassment can be between two individuals or it may involve groups of people. It might be obvious or it might be insidious. It may be persistent or an isolated incident. It can also occur in written communications, by phone or through email, not just face-to-face.*

70   Although I have used the term Control Freak Management, the definition from Wikipedia **(para 446 – 449)** which described the management practice in my former college. A softer

definition would be "Micro-managing." I believe that there is considerable evidence that this culture pervades the Secretariat and beyond. Under a heading: "Group Targets Staff Bullies, *Director Graham Bennett told the (2007 CG) AGM that reported instances of bullying had dropped by three percentage points to 18% who had contributed to the CG's confidential Talkback initiative." Co-op News 29 May 2007*

71   From this statistic, nearly 20% of staff had reported bullying. As there is currently 90.000 staff, if the same statistic applies, a staggering 18,000 staff are bullied, suggesting bullying is endemic.

72   Often, alleging of a breach of confidentiality is a strategy used to silence or intimidate members, which goes against the Co-op principles of openness and free speech. This controversial issue is raised in the section: Confidentiality, "A Noose to Hang Dissenters?"

73   Apparently, Karen Froggatt, through her actions, wanted to control information and suppress anything that might reflect badly upon CG. For example, in her email (Ref 2, p1) she states: "It is customary for me to produce and circulate notes of these (Chairs) meetings." [I.e. to control information, although this "policy" was not stated]. She went on: "… I avoid going into detail about any sensitive issues." **[To protect Management, although she was later prepared to vilify and name me in Regional Board Minutes].**

74   Area Committee Secretary (Collette Harber) also appeared to want to protect Management, as she did not like to Minute negative criticism. It took three meetings to get a Health and Safety issue minuted after a store visit. If my concerns had been taken up, the CG could have saved itself £500,000 as it was fined for the very issues I raised. It is an example of the contempt committee members were held by the Secretariat.

75   Karen Froggatt used to write all the speeches for speakers at meetings. I was totally unaware of this. When, on one occasion, I was to address a Half Yearly members meeting, it dropped through my door the day before. She did not consult with me as to content whatsoever. Although she might argue that she was being "helpful," she was treating speakers like ventriloquists dummies as she was controlling the information. Clearly, she was attempting to do this at the Half Yearly meeting I was to chair, by refusing to copy my, and others' articles, for a presentation. For this incident, I reported her conduct to Nick Eyre, (Company Secretary) **(see Appendix, para 366 - 393).**

76   Under the heading: "Background – Co-operative Group Structure" the FSA letter (below) also gives a brief outline of the democratic tiers and published critical voices suggesting that they are weak. **[This has been transferred into Governance (para 259)].**

77   Under the heading "My Case," I detail the bullying, harassment and victimisation I suffered at the hands of the Secretariat and The Regional Board.

78   There appeared to be a personal vendetta waged against me by Regional Secretary (Karen Froggatt) and Regional Board Chair (Adrienne Lowe), although others were involved. Their motive appears to have been to silence me and resentment about my extensive publications in the Co-op News. To my knowledge, it must be unprecedented for the attacks on me by Regional Board to be minuted. These meetings were conducted in secret without my knowledge. Thus, members were culpable in the bullying. Neither was I given an opportunity to defend myself against allegations from Karen Froggatt and Adrienne Lowe.

79   Nick Eyre (Company Secretary) and his deputy (Moira Lees) were fully aware of what had taken place. As Lawyers, they would know the meaning of "Natural Justice," but they appear to have disregarded the principle, which would go against lawyers' ethics.

80   *"In English law, **natural justice** is technical terminology for the rule against bias and the right to a fair hearing. While the term natural justice is often retained as a general concept, it has largely been replaced and extended by the more general "duty to act fairly". Wikipedia 1 Feb 2014*

81   **FSA CO-OPERATIVE AND MUTUAL DIVISION STATEMENT OF COMPLAINT.**

Note: This document is based upon a letter sent to the FSA in 2007, but with updating and minor editing.

82   I am making this formal complaint against The Co-operative Group, New Century House, MANCHESTER, M60 4ES for three reasons:
- For the FSA to look critically at the way the democratic structure operates and to address the considerable widespread concern that the Co-operative Group (henceforth called CG) is failing to comply with the fundamental principles upon which it is founded.
- To try and get some form of justice for the way I have been treated, which has implications for other elected members, who have very few rights or protection.
- To try and ensure that a system of support/advice, grievance, independent arbitration/mediation and appeal is implemented within the Group especially for elected representatives.

83   **INTRODUCTION**

84   This document attempts to describe the bullying, victimisation and harassment I have experienced as Chair of an Area Committee, by the Group's Secretariat and the SE Regional Board. From my sources, other elected members have had similar experiences. This fear of being attacked undermines their function and duty to hold Management to account, as directors and Area Committee members. In a sense, my experience is a case study. I believe the evidence shows that I was attacked and targeted by the Secretariat from the Company Secretary to the Regional Area Committee Secretary. Their apparent motive is because I am outspoken, write critical articles and letters. Thus, their goal was to silence and/or oust me.

85   The first section headed, **"BACKGROUND,"** is intended to provide some insight to a reader who is unfamiliar with the CG's structure, current issues and problems. It provides independent evidence that underlines and supports my view that it is dysfunctional, undemocratic and unrepresentative of members. **[This has been transferred into Governance (para 259)].**

86   The second section, headed **MY CASE,** outlines the attack upon myself. Initially, this was by the Regional Secretary, Karen Froggatt. In a document she presented to the Regional Board [**without my knowledge** (Dec 2005)], she made allegations against me. The **Appendix, entitled "In Defence of Integrity and Character,"** is my detailed defence, presented to my Area Committee before a June 2006 "disciplinary" hearing, which highlights the allegations and my rebuttal in the "comments."

87 Some of my articles are attached, particularly "Project Exchequer" **(Ref 1, p1)**. For brevity, I have provided only occasional originals of extracts from letters in the Co-operative News, which supported my views. The references 1 – 16 and the Appendix entitled: "In Defence of Integrity and Character" provide supporting evidence of how the Secretariat victimised, harassed and bullied me. They also show the bias of the Regional Board in condemning me, without hearing any defence from me, by giving unqualified support for the Regional Secretary. Thus its members were culpable. Relevant parts are highlighted.

88 **MY CASE (From FSA letter)**

89 I am making this complaint as my only recourse for justice and to help the Co-operative Group become more democratic with greater protection for elected representatives. As evidenced below, we have a Control Freak Management Culture, which undermines what Co-operation stands for - openness, democracy, caring for others, free speech.

90 I serve as an elected representative on an Area Committee and I feel that I have been unjustly and shabbily treated by the Secretariat and the South East Regional Board. In October 2004 my committee elected me Chair to try and stand up to the Secretariat, which undermines the basic principle of a Co-operative - owned and run by its members. I am no longer Chair after being forced to stand down, summer 2006, because of false allegations made by the senior South East Regional Official, Karen Froggett (Regional Secretary). Recently, a high level source alleged to me that bullying was rife on the Main Board. Geraint Day reinforces that view:

91 *" ... in a number of societies there have been instances of bullying behaviour, defamation, vindictiveness or sheer unwillingness to accept collective responsibility. The result can be that some colleagues might fear to participate at all. Maybe these situations contribute to the cases where directors do not contribute to meetings for fear of being bullied, intimidated or embarrassed .....for them to occur in a co-operative is shameful." Geraint Day (Director and Co-op Party NEC) News 28 June -12 July 2005.* **Bullying, silencing critics, controlling people and information, are central characteristics of a Control Freak Management culture, which pervades the CG. An example was an attempt by Karen Froggett to "control" me by, implicitly, alleging a breach of confidentiality 6 Apr 05 (Ref 2 p.1 & 2).**

92 As my Area Committee's Chair, I had attended a Regional Chairs' meeting. Karen Froggatt criticised me for writing and circulating a report I wrote for my Area Committee, normal practice. I pointed out that it went only to my Area Committee and those who attended the meeting. It appears that she had resented me doing this as her email explicitly states; *"It is customary for me to produce and circulate notes of these meetings."* **Thus she is attempting to control the information to be made available.** Although she claims that she was acting on the instruction of the Regional Board, it is very easy for her (as Regional Secretary) to influence it, even if behind the scenes (important when reviewing her allegations in Appendix, later). Added to this, the then Chair was Bob Harber whose wife, as Area Committee Secretary, was at the centre of *the "sensitive information in your notes."* From my report's complete extract **(Ref 3 p. 1 & 2),** this was trivial as it did not mention names:

93 *"4d It appears that a Kent committee had a rather "heated" exchange at one of their meetings. I cannot recall one on our committee, even though we sometimes have different views. The suggestion was that the Chair should adjourn to let things cool down."*

94 A report circulated around all Area Committees by another attendee (Brian Constable) was

described as a "mistake," by Karen Froggatt in her email in reply **(Ref 2, p 1 & 2).** As far as I know, he was not censored and I was thus being singled out and victimised.

95 Using confidentiality appears to be a tactic to silence critics and outspoken elected members. The late Hugh Bridge was suspended for three months on those grounds and, presumably, Karen Froggatt was behind his suspension – further evidence of her wishing to exercise control.

96 I have suffered considerable anguish from, in my view, this abusive and bullying Secretariat, for writing articles, being outspoken and a perceived as a "dissident" and, perhaps, a threat to Management's power. I had many articles published in the Co-operative News, critical of management or suggesting "radical" ideas, particularly giving power and decision making to ordinary members (perhaps through some form of referenda). My Project Exchequer article 2005 **(Ref 1 p 1),** critical of cuts to be imposed on the democratic structures and other external co-operative organisations, helped provoke a storm of protest from members against the cuts, as seen above **[moved to Governance para 266 – 268].** It contributed towards a backlash against the Management's and Secretariat's proposals. I understand my article caused considerable Secretariat fury. Soon afterwards, I was accused of breaching confidentiality involving extensive correspondence with the Regional Secretary and Company Secretary (Nick Eyre). I believe that the Senior Secretariat set out to frighten, intimidate, bully, neutralise and/or oust me.

97 In an email 11 Aug 05 **(Ref 5),** Karen Froggatt began the attack when she accused me of a breach of confidentiality by writing my article (on Project Exchequer). This was followed by a letter 2 Sep 05, which demanded that I admit my "guilt" **(Ref 6).** In a sense, she was asking me to "incriminate" myself. My letter in reply (7 Sep 05) asked her to identify what **was** the "breach." She did not reply. Soon afterwards, Nick Eyre (Company Secretary) took over the attack upon me. After protracted correspondence on this and other matters (30 letters in total) he finally admitted that the only issue was that Euro Co-op was not aware that they were to receive a cut in funding (and I only have his word that there was a breach). This seemed disproportionate to the "offence." As it was, I had taken reasonable steps to ensure that Project Exchequer was in the Public Domain at the time of writing. My article was published about four months after Project Exchequer was announced.

98 Since the Secretariat failed to brow beat me on this issue, another line of attack opened up. This came in the form of a document circulated around the Regional Board and, later, my Area Committee (approximately 30 elected people). It is possible that it went further afield. I totally refuted the allegations. This document appeared about one month after I had formally complained about Karen Froggatt's conduct to the Company Secretary, Nick Eyre. She had refused to carry out my reasonable request, regarding the Half Yearly meeting I was to Chair. This was to copy my article and allow me to use my slides to aid a presentation I intended to make on Project Exchequer's cuts She had also threatened to (implicitly) undermine me at the meeting **(see Appendix, para 366– 393).** It appeared that "attack was being used as a means of defence" to offset my complaint about **her.** *b) Retaliation: the bully counter attacks. The bully quickly and seamlessly follows the denial with an aggressive counter-attack of counter-criticism or counter-allegation, often based on distortion or fabrication* **(Definition para 448).**

99 I was unaware of Karen Froggatt's document until the Regional Board had passed a motion fully supporting her. This was quoted in Nick Eyre's (Company Secretary's) letter 9 May 2006 **(Ref 9, p 1).** Note that Karen Froggatt sits on the Regional Board, in a position to influence the meeting and writes the Minutes.

100 ***The Regional Board considered a paper produced by the Regional Secretary, outlining her***

concerns regarding the behaviour of Vie Parks, Chair of the Surrey & Berkshire Area Committee.

101 *The matter was discussed in detail. The content of the Regional Secretary's paper was noted with deep concern. A motion expressing support for, and full confidence in, the Regional Secretary and the Membership Team was proposed and was adopted unanimously.*

102   *It was agreed that Surrey & Berks Area Committee would be asked to give detailed consideration to the matters raised by the Regional Secretary at the earliest opportunity, and report back to the Regional Board on their views and on any action to be taken in respect of the issues raised.*

103 They had not heard my side of the story and condemned me solely on the Regional Secretary's allegations. She sent me an email dated 21 December 2005 **(Ref 7)** containing the Minutes (which she writes) and her document containing her allegations. This was the first I had heard of this and the decisions (and judgements) which Regional Board members had made in secrecy and without my knowledge. In so doing, it showed a bias and a contravention of "natural Justice." Karen Froggatt, although subject to my formal complaint against her to Nick Eyre (her Boss), she was **left in post and in a position, as Secretary to the Regional Board, to influence its outcomes.** Procedurally, this appeared to be utterly wrong.1 ought to say that the allegations against me came from other senior employees in the Membership hierarchy, indicating that there was some form of "conspiracy" to concoct "evidence" to smear my name, as an excuse to instigate some form of disciplinary proceedings in support of a fellow member of the Management Team.

104 Under the rules, my Area Committee had the power (with no right of appeal) to suspend or "discipline" me. I had provided a defence refuting Karen Froggatt's claims **(Appendix para 331 - 445)** which they saw. Although I believe that a good number did not believe her allegations, they were under immense pressure from Nick Eyre and his deputy, Moira Lees, to find against me. Indeed, although against the rules, the Vice Chair of the Regional Board (Mike Hedgethorn, another senior manager) was sent to our Area Committee meeting to "observe." I objected to him being there but after, I am told, heated debate by the Committee in private, he was allowed to stay. He is a very strong, assertive personality, who was plainly influencing and pressurising the meeting stating, "I want this dealt with tonight!" He also commented and made statements at other times. Procedurally, this was wrong. He was certainly not just an "observer," perhaps a sort of gauleiter.

105 Our Area Committee had wasted about three, possibly four monthly meetings discussing the whole issue, which paralysed our Committee's normal business. The outcome was that I had to stand down as Chair on the ground that I had not carried out the Area Committee's instruction in a previous meeting to write a letter and bring closure **(this is Minuted, Ref 8).** [This states that the decision was "unanimous" but three members told me afterwards that this was not true, as they had "fought for me."] I felt that I should not apologise for something the Regional Secretary had created and writing a document **(Appendix)** that was untrue. Later, I was privately told, that the Area Committee was being threatened with sanctions if they did not find against me (suspension?). It is significant that no reference was made to Karen Froggatt's document or my defence. Thus, they appeared not to accept Karen Froggatt's allegations as being true.

106 For me, this episode in my life was highly stressful, depressing and full of anguish, resulting in considerable loss of face and damage to my reputation. It is utterly wrong that a senior staff member can make unfounded allegations, with the Secretariat behind her. To my knowledge, Karen Froggatt's allegations were not questioned and assumed to be true. In a tribunal or Court of Law,

© **Vic Parks 2014**

Allegations are made, a Defence is entered and witnesses are cross-examined. Karen Froggatt's Line Manager (Moira Lees) and ultimate boss, Nick Eyre (Company Secretary) were lawyers and had disregarded "Natural Justice." This appears to say little about their Co-operative ethics. Implicitly, I drew their attention to this and the injustice in my reply 12 May to his letter 9 May 2006:

107 *Dear Nick,   Thank you for your letter dated 9 May 2006.*

108 *With regard to the quotations from Regional Board Minutes, these motions were passed without any representation on my part either written or oral. Clearly, as Karen Froggatt is the Secretary to the Regional Board it would seem inappropriate, prejudicial and unjust for her to sit in on those meetings when she is making allegations against me. It could be argued that it was a misuse of her position to gain an advantage. In addition, the Chair of the Regional Board (Adrienne Lowe) is a party to the allegations made in Karen Froggatt's document. This is the part referring to the Regional Principles and Values meeting, which she chaired at the time. As you are fully aware, Karen's document came after my formal complaint to YOU about HER behaviour towards me. Indeed, I feel very strongly that it I who is being bullied and undermined in my role as Chair. Karen has sought to involve members of the management in trying to build a case against me. This is why I feel that arbitration from an outside, independent body or individual is necessary. As I understand it, there are no laid down rules or Regulations for the current circumstances we are in. IS THIS THE CASE?*

109 *I have to say, that the impasse with regard to the mediator is also on your side and not solely upon mine, as implied in the wording of your letter. Implicitly, you have refused my offer of approaching Co-operatives UK or Alan Middleton who is widely respected throughout the Co-operative Movement as being impartial. I do not feel, in the circumstances of ad hoc arrangements, that I will get a fair hearing, especially if the matter goes back before the Regional Board. By making its statement, which you quote, it could be argued that it has prejudiced itself in any future hearings of the allegations on both sides.*

110 *I would also comment on Liaquat Lal that in my conversation with him he WAS vague about the date and what was said. As he said, "It was a long time ago." It was certainly more than "some months" [in Karen Froggatt's allegations] and was well over a year perhaps two. I have to say that if this is placed in the Public Domain, the fact that an educational manager is prepared to "Give evidence against a "Student" has considerable consequences for trust between tutors and students. As a Teacher Trainer, trust is an important prerequisite between teachers and students. Non-prejudicial debate and discussion in training sessions is very important. As I recall when I attended a Summer School at Wyboston some three years ago, Liaquat was drinking and socialising with the students. If "evidence is being taken down and may be used against a student" this has considerable implications for future educational events.*

111 ***I note that you have not answered my questions in my last letter and I re-list them below. I would appreciate a prompt reply as I am in the process of drawing up a statement rebutting Karen's allegations***

112 *In the circumstances (especially in view of the threat of litigation), am I entitled to legal representation?*

113 *What support is available for elected representatives? Clearly, I am disadvantaged since you are a lawyer and Moira Lees and Karen Froggatt are highly conversant with "The Rules" and their interpretation, since that is part of their job.*

114 *As an elected representative, do I have indemnity (e.g. insurance) to cover a potential claim against me?*

115 *Clearly state what damage the article did.*

116 *How is Colette involved in the dispute (reference top of your page 2, 3 March letter)?*

117 *Were you and/or Moira Lees fully aware of the steps Karen was taking at each stage of this dispute?*

118 *I note that there is a proposed Rule change at the SGM, with regard to indemnifying directors and officers Rule 181. Should not this apply to members on elected bodies, in the interest of equality?*

119 *I suggest that in the circumstances - the high level of allegations on both sides- against Regional Secretary and an Area committee Chair, and the prejudicial decisions of the Regional Board and Karen's role on it, that an independent body outside the Co-operative Group hears the dispute. It is clear from your letter that we are moving towards a formal hearing.* **(Ref 9 p. 2 &3).**

120 His letter in reply ignored my questions, as I am sure he would have difficulty answering them. Instead he issued a threat:

121 *"If you really insist on raking over your actions in detail and force the issues, I do not think from my attendance at the South East Board meeting, that you enjoy support in your Regional Board and your are aware of the concerns that have been raised by staff concerning your behaviour."* **(Ref 9, p. 4)**

122 Regional Board's hostility was evident in his reply. As to what **was** my "behaviour," it is only that described by the Regional Secretary's false allegations. As can be seen from my subsequent correspondence with the Chair, she would (or could not) define my "bad" conduct **(Ref 10 p. 1, 2, 3).** Clearly, the Regional Board members are biased, in its willingness to unconditionally support the Regional Secretary's allegations, without examining the "evidence." It was said to me that the Chair (Adrienne Lowe) "is looking to give me a public hanging, and is watching every move I make."

123 Although battered by the above, I was not going to let the bullies shut me up. I wrote an article which was published over two pages of B4: "It's Your Choice … A Blueprint for the future…or the Final Curtain for Co-op Democracy?" 25 July 2006 **(Ref 11 p. 1 & 2).** I was trying to explore the issues that the Quinquennial Review ought to address. I suspected from previous experience, there would be "huff and puff" and a CON(&)INSULTation, but things would carry on as before .**Those in power would not reform themselves and the Secretariat writes the rule changes, if any, in its favour [and probably so even after Kelly and Myners' reviews].**

124 The worst outcome was the confidentiality rules. Although unpublished, I wrote a critique called: "The Code of Conduct – A Noose to Hang Dissenters?" as it would give even more powers of control to The Secretariat **(See Confidentiality section para 149 - 235).** The Review was deferred to 2007/8 because of the merger with United but the outcome was more or less as I predicted: little change other than the "Age Rule" being abolished.

125 The Regional Board passed motions behind my back and, yet again, its Chair, Adrienne Lowe, attacked me publicly in the Co-operative News 22 Aug 2006 because of my 25 July 2006 article:

126 *"At a recent meeting of the Co-operative Group Southeast Regional Board, member noted with concern, and indeed some alarm, the article by Vie Parks in the Co-operative News (July 20) and the prominence given to his highly personal views. Vic presents a negative and potentially demoralising account of what we believe will be a root and branch reviews of the Group's democratic structures and practices ..... We as a Board, do not consider ourselves to be "powerless" or that "consultation is often just a sham."* **(Ref 12).**

127 Adrienne Lowe's statement was in contrast to the published views expressed regarding the Democratic Deficit, in the Governance section **(para 262 – 268)** and the fact that the SE Regional Board failed to stop the cuts under Project Exchequer, even though the three SE Main Board Directors wrote to their Main Board Chair. Neither did they stop the controversial closure of the flagship non-food departmental stores.

128 Colin Richell [still an AC member] criticised her for attacking me, despite us having conflicting views on other issues. It is worth noting that he appears to identify a "witch hunt" against me:

129 *(Heading)**Free speech vital:*** *I feel uneasy that the Chair of the South East Regional Board should write to the News to protest about comments made by Vic Parks (July 25th). Mr Parks was clearly writing in a personal capacity and he, like many members, is unhappy with some of the current policies of the Co-op Group. ... I am concerned that there appears to be a 'witch hunt' against some outspoken members (not me I hasten to add) and this should not happen in a democratic organisation. Why must criticism result in accusations that the critics are not working to the same objectives? Collin Richell, 5 – 19 Sep 2006* **(Ref 13)**

130 In April 2007, as delegate, I spoke at the Special General Meeting dealing with the Merger of Group and United Co-operatives. Adrienne Lowe (RB Chair) publicly attacked me again in this meeting, claiming that she had the Regional Board's support, although it had not met prior to her mounting the attack. Yet again, the Regional Board attacked me Minutes 28 June 2007:

131 *Further to discussion at the previous meeting regarding Vic Parks' conduct, the Regional Secretary referred to legal advice she had received between meetings regarding course of action proposed.*

132 *The Regional Board recalled the matters of concern most recently, i.e.*

> • ***Vic Parks' conduct at the Group SGM, where he had disregarded the action agreed by the delegation at the pre-meeting and where his conduct*** *had led to the Regional Chair speaking to disassociate the Region from his comments.*
> • ***His letter to Co-op News in April 2007,*** *which it was felt had reflected negatively on the Regional Board and management.*
> • *It was noted that due to pressures on the Regional Board agenda, action in this respect had been carried forward to the following meeting, at which Vic's conduct at the SGM was also considered.*
> • ***The Regional Board stressed that it did not wish to restrict freedom of speech,*** *though it felt that it was essential that regional delegates should agree (and adhere to) a collective course of action, and that all delegates should conduct themselves in an appropriate manner.*
> • *Discussion took place regarding the way forward in respect of the ongoing concern regarding Vic Parks' conduct. It was agreed that instead of initiating formal proceedings under the Code of Conduct,* ***the Regional Board would ask Surrey and Berkshire Area Committee to note the Regional Boards concerns and to cease selecting Vic Parks as one of their delegates to an major conferences/events for a fixed period.*** *It was agreed that the Minute outlining the Regional Board's deliberations in this respect would be communicated to members of Surrey and Berkshire Area Committee would be able to convey the Regional Boards concerns to their colleagues on the Area Committee.* **(Ref 14)**

133 It appears my "conduct at the Group SGM" was to **ask questions** and raise issues. **I thought**

that was the role of delegates? For outsiders, use of the words: "conduct" and "concerns" conjure up negative images of rage and violence. Managers who wish to subjugate or sack staff try to build a "case," even if a series of trivial "crimes" or just plain lies. Metaphorically, or physically, the evidence is stored in filing cabinets and the drawers are opened when the managers feel that the time is right. Having seen such managers emotionally destroy staff in my former college, I am very much aware of their strategies. It is Classical Control Freak Management. I understand that at least two of Karen Froggett's staff left after instigating Grievance Procedures, although they settled before going to formal tribunal. I was very careful not to conduct myself in a way that could be used against me. It is hypocritical of CG to state that it has a zero tolerance on bullying, yet it does not seem to extend this to elected representatives. That is why legislation is needed to protect them from not only Management, but their so-called "colleagues."

134 Presumably, Adrienne Lowe was responsible for the Minute: that I *"... had disregarded the action agreed by the delegation at the pre-meeting, and where his conduct had led to the Regional Chair speaking, to disassociate the Region from his comments."* I cannot recall having done this. However, I clearly remember at the pre-meeting that she had said: "You can express your personal views and ask questions." Thus, I believe that she was being untruthful. Looking back, was it a trap? I did as she said, but was publicly humiliated in the meeting. It is worth noting that another SE delegate had asked questions and made statements from the floor (a retired SE Regional Secretary), but **he** was not singled out. At the bottom of my SGM report to my Area Committee **(Ref 15, p.2)** it states: "I made it clear that the views I expressed were mine and I was raising issues raised by my Area Committee and not the SE delegations." This was dated 1 May 2007, two months before the Regional Board's Minuted condemnation of me. By this time, it was common practice to do this behind my back without being asked for any defence. From the report, it appears that my emails to my Area Committee members had been leaked: "My emails to our AC the week prior to the SGM appear to have been circulated to high levels, with Nick Eyre (Company Secretary) replying to them. It also appears, from a remark of Bob Harber, that they went around Regional Board."

135 In the June Minutes reference was made, **yet again,** to my article 25 July 2006, for which Adrienne Lowe attacked me in the press **(para 126 & Ref 12).** Hypocritically, "they did not want to restrict freedom of speech," yet it is clear that their whole campaign was to do just that! Karen Froggett writes the Minutes and can ingest her prejudices or manipulate them to help build a "case" against me. Note also that the minutes state that my Area Committee should "...cease selecting Vic Parks as one of their delegates to any major conferences/events for a fixed period." This was one of the straws in my decision to leave about a year later.

136 It was also becoming difficult for me to get published in the Co-op News (funded and pressurised by CG). As with many writers, we try to change the world for the better, to fight injustice and fight for principles. I could live with the general ostracization within the CG (probably due to false rumours and a campaign to discredit me), but I felt that I had become influentially impotent. Added to this, I had been seriously ill after a leg operation, catching MSSA. I had fought hard, taking a great deal of Psychological pain, injustice and humiliation, but they had achieved their end of ousting me. However, sometimes, one has to let things go.

137 In my SGM report, **(Ref 15)** I stated that Peter Begley (former CG Main Board director, SW Region) pointed out the immorality of Peter Marks being guaranteed CEO, the delegation system as being nonsensical and United changing its rules to borrow ten times its assets (borrowed £M210?). All of this may have a bearing on the Co-op Bank collapse. I raised these issues because: "If nothing else, a benchmark had been registered." (Prophetic?). In a CG

national Half Yearly Meeting, five months later, the delegate (former SE RB Director) states: "As these were relatively minor matters in the context of the question and resolution, I felt it unnecessary to push the point **but I can imagine how frustrated Vic must have felt on a previous occasion with matters of greater import.**" BJM 7/11/07

138 I believe that these personal attacks (much against Co-operative principles), using the weight of the Regional Board, are unprecedented. Clearly, it was personal and the Chair's hostility to me was evident soon after I first met her many years ago on the Regional Values and Principles Committee. Another Regional Board member, Bob Harber was the former Chair. Although he had attempted to bully me and berate me at an Area Committee Conference around 2002, after I had had another article published. His animosity towards me was also probably due to me highlighting the issue of him (as Chair) being married to the second most SE senior officer, the Area Committee Secretary. I (with the support of others) had raised this with (Company Secretary) Nick Eyre as a potential conflict of interest, prior to the appearance of my Project Exchequer article. His enquiries showed that the three SE regional Main Board directors agreed that "there was a problem." (This is documented in correspondence with Nick Eyre). Bob Harber's wife later made an allegation against me in Karen Froggatt's document **(Appendix).** Many Area Committees found her difficult to deal with. She had also expressed animosity towards me and tried to undermine me as Chair, in meetings (See Chairs report, **(Ref 3, p1 4d)** and the Appendix headed: Collette Harber's Conduct **(para 429 - 435).** Recently, a member of Kent Committee said that she had walked out of a meeting and that is why the meeting was "heated" in Ref 3, 4d.

139 The Regional Board's prejudice is clearly evident in the Chair's correspondence with me **(Ref 10, p. 1, 2, 3).** From my experience in voluntary Public Service and politics, one acquires enemies, for sometimes frivolous reasons. Because of the criticism in the Minutes, it is plain that some members of Regional Board resented my many articles and letters published in the Co-operative Press, over the years. Added to this, I am critical of the weak democracy and the impotence of the elected members, which reflect the views expressed by others **(see para 262 – 268).** Perhaps they disliked me exposing their relatively weak position in influencing change.

140 It could be argued that the whole affair was a personal vendetta carried out by two individuals who appeared to be very good friends, and allies, who appeared to abuse their positions. Other members with personal prejudices probably joined in the attacks. Karen Froggatt wrote the Regional Board Minutes and was in an "advisory." This gave her considerable power and influence, sitting in the meetings. Equally, the Chair is a strong personality and, allegedly, berates committee members. As many who sit on committees are quislings, "nodding donkeys" or just plainly indifferent, few put their heads above the parapet. In extreme cases like mine, those who "ask the questions others would like to ask but don't," swing on the metaphorical gibbet as a warning to others who might step out of line and "rock the boat." Instead of covertly doing things behind my back, Karen Froggatt's concerns should have been raised with me in the first instance. However, she appears not to have wanted to do this as the documentation shows that her "agenda" was to be punitive, and she needed to try and build a "case" against me.

141 Although some elected members agreed with my views, they were reluctant to openly support me, either through fear or by having "vested interests"; for example, by being deeply involved in (or running) Co-operative organisations dependent upon Group funding (e.g. Credit Unions, Woodcraft Folk, Co-op Party, etc.). Main and Regional Board directors have considerable salaries and are bound by "corporate responsibility." Clearly, being associated with a "dissident" could damage them. As several staff said to me: "I shouldn't be seen talking to

you." However, Len Wardle did come up to me at a SE AGM and said "I don't mind being seen talking to you!" But then, he was Main Board Chair and I had known him for many years.

142 **CONCLUSION AND RECOMMENDATIONS.**

143 I believe that I have made a case that what I have suffered is Classic Control Freak Management strategies **(Appendix)** i.e. harassment, intimidation and bullying. I have witnessed and experienced this in my former employment as a Senior Lecturer in Teacher Training. Members of staff were deliberately demoralised, victimised and emotionally destroyed. I left because my role as Teacher Trainer was to build people up yet management was knocking them down. I was also a "target" as an "expensive" Senior Lecturer and being outspoken; so took premature Early Retirement.

144 Nick Eyre (Company Secretary and solicitor) was fully aware of what was happening as we had had considerable correspondence (some 30 letters) and appears to be behind the attack on me or, at least, advising the Regional Secretary through his deputy, Moira Lees. It is my view that the Secretariat, starting at the Company Secretary set out to neutralise, bully, threaten and/or oust me. Characteristically, these are the traits of a Control Freak management culture.

145 Usually, management initiatives go through "on the nod." Instead, my articles helped wake up the membership, causing considerable Secretariat fury. Clearly, the whole saga was an attempt to silence me and deter others from putting their "heads above the parapet."

146 My reason for my FSA complaint was to expose the injustice and precarious situations Group elected members are in. Taking on the might of an £9B turn over company is very daunting, since elected members have few rights compared with employees. Although staff have access to unions, legal advice and protected by Employment Law lay, elected members have no such support. After being a long distance Litigant in Person for many years (including getting permission for and acting in the Court of Appeal, no mean feat) I know the consequences - drain on my emotions and well-being. Elected members cannot carry out their proper function of holding the Management/Secretariat to account in an atmosphere of fear, similar to the Enron, Mid-Staffordshire, Colchester scandals.

147 I had suggested to Nick Eyre that there should be an outside mediator. At first Moira Lees, the Regional Secretary's line manager, was offered. This was totally unacceptable to me since she was directly or indirectly party to the dispute and prejudiced. I suggested Alan Middleton, a well-respected senior person in the Co-operative Movement but outside of the CG structure, but this was refused **(Ref 9, p.2).** I would also comment on the fact that communications from the Senior Secretariat often came very late. At my disciplinary meeting with my Area Committee (June 2006), Moira Lees contacted the acting Chair just an hour or so beforehand. In my view, this is tantamount to cheap lawyers' tricks when they serve documents going through the doors of the Court, to unbalance the other side. The Group hierarchy put immense pressure on my Area Committee to find against me.

148 There needs to be proper Grievance procedures for elected members, giving equal rights and protection, as enjoyed by staff, with an independent appeals tribunal **(see Respect Works para 60 - 69).** Added to this, there needs to be independent support and legal advice, which could be provided by a trade union or association. In my letter, dated 12 May 2006 **(Ref 9, p3),** I sought advice and information on these matters but they were ignored by Nick Eyre. Obviously, it was in their interest for me to be weak when they were carrying out their bullying. All this, was to put me at a considerable disadvantage.

© **Vic Parks 2014**

CONFIDENTIALITY

The Code of Conduct: A Noose to Hang Dissenters?

149 **CONFIDENTIALITY** is used by the Secretariat to control people and stop them speaking out. As stated in my OVERVIEW, what **is** confidential is defined by the Secretariat and is a form of censorship. As stated previously, the Secretariat appears to be obsessed with secrecy and wishes to "control everything," a trait of a Control Freak Management style. This section is based on a paper/article I wrote analysing the CG Code of Conduct (2006). It was a revised version of the 2003/4 Code and appears to close loop holes and become yet more controlling after my institutional bullying in 2005/6.

150 It would appear that procedures and parts of the 2003/4 Code in force at the time were ignored, yet should have applied to my situation. It has to be remembered that the Rules, Code, policies, etc., are written by the Secretariat and biased in its favour. Although the elected members may, theoretically, have the final say, the reality is that they are just "nodded through." Invariably, there is little time to scrutinise the implications and hold in-depth discussions. What is agreed at Area Committee level has little bearing on what is passed at a SGM. Because of the Delegate System **[criticized in the Governance section, para 261)** it is easy to control its view and voting intentions by controlling groups.

151 The Code makes it easy for the Secretariat to attack outspoken members. One interpretation is that it no one could speak to anyone outside a committee. **This has serious consequences for Governance.** Because of the importance for training members from different committees in a region and nationally, sharing experience and knowledge, is essential. I understand that there is a recent case of it being used to discipline an elected member, which indicates little has changed since my involvement with CG.

152 **This was the draft article written 2008. Its arguments and analyses are just as pertinent now as then.**

153 *THE CODE OF CONDUCT – A NOOSE TO HANG DISSENTERS*

154 *In my letter dated News 10-24 June 2008, I challenged the Group Board to put its Constitutional Review proposals to the whole membership, as a referendum. I sent the draft, an article, to the Review Committee as a formal submission. Apart from an acknowledgement, my proposals were ignored. That was not surprising when even the views of Pauline Green (CEO Co-operatives UK) carried-little weight. Her wish for some form of one member one vote News Jan/ Feb 2008) went also unheeded. What chance, then, of me influencing the "good and the great"?! Perhaps a referendum of all the elected members might have been more acceptable. Recently, the Constitutional Review proposals were passed at the SGM, subject to further huffing and puffing later in the year. With the tempting "compensation payments," it is likely that influential members will be blinded by the potential "bling." Many may decide "enough is enough" and give up trying to keep the Co-operative ideals of the early pioneers alive against the might of Management and its influential, member quislings.*

155 *Yet, I beg those who still have power to influence outcomes to look at their legacy, for the future integrity of the Co-operative Movement. The World is facing turbulent times. Co-*

operation is a positive alternative to Totalitarian states, deepening social and economic chaos even with the possibility of a Third World War because of burgeoning populations, ever decreasing resources, global warming and so on. For the world outside (especially politicians), the Co-operative Group is a test bed for what could be seen as "Corporate Co-operation." The core principle, owned and controlled by its members, is now little more than a fig leaf. It has been well argued for many years that elected members (especially lower tier) are really just wasting their time. In perhaps five or ten years' time, there is a real danger of the Co-operative democracy being a withered skeleton, dead on its feet. What is the point of proclaiming the merits of Co-operation (a fundamental tenet of the Co-operative Party) when the Group's members (the owners) have fewer rights than shareholders in Corporate Capitalism (PLCs)?

156 *Potentially, the final extinguishing of co-operative democracy is in the draft proposals for the elected members' Code of Conduct. This will be a noose around the necks of each elected member, from top to bottom. It will be jerked when members step from the official line or go off-message. Confidentiality will be used as a weapon to extinguish outspoken and dissident voices, undermining the principle of free speech, the bedrock of effective Democracy.*

157 *Elected members must closely analyse the implications of the Code of Conduct. Much of it is subjective and open to interpretation. An elected member would need to be a lawyer to understand the potential minefield he/she would operate in. In the absence of independent, external tribunals (which employees have access to) elected members will be torn to bits by probably prejudiced internal "panels." If allegations of misconduct come from Management (as in the past), the contest will be heavily biased as Management will have access to unlimited legal knowledge and resources to be pitched against any puny, isolated individual. In my article News 19 Feb - 4 Mar 2008 I argued for support for elected members through, for example, a trade union. Those proposals were unheeded by the Constitutional Review. With the draft Code the need for protection and support is even greater.*

158 *THE CODE - A critique.*

159 *My analysis of the CG Code of Conduct is based upon documents circulated at the time. I guess little has been revised and, if it has, I suspect that it will be a further "tightening of the noose."*

160 *The Group's Code of Conduct for Disciplinary proceedings against elected members has no right of appeal, whereas staff could go to an Industrial Tribunal. The only appeal would be a Judicial Review in the High Court. However, that would be unlikely. An elected member would have to be very determined, deeply aggrieved or perhaps stupid to take on the might of a £12B turnover company, with its unlimited legal resources. He/she would risk very substantial costs as the losing party.*

161 *There has been a case where The Group went for costs against a deceased, losing elected member's estate. Perhaps in the interest of fairness, in the current system, a member should have the right to appeal a disciplinary decision to the High Court. If the Group loses it would normally pay the member's costs. However, if the elected member was unsuccessful, Group would undertake that each party would pay its own costs. This would help offset a highly inequitable situation especially if the elected member acted as a Litigant in Person.*

162 *Throughout the code, it states that: "members should seek guidance from the Area Committee Secretary or Regional Secretary." This may be reasonable providing it is guidance rather than a direct order. One of the major problems of modern Co-operation is whether staff are the servants or masters. Ideally, they should co-operate as a team but long Co-operative history highlights the "Them and Us" situation. Would the guidance offered be in the self-interest of Management or the legitimate position? Officers are sometimes accused of defending or excusing Management. Because of the way the Code is worded, the Secretariat becomes the "Police" (some say the KGB!). Clearly, by the then Regional Secretary refusing to carry out my instruction as Chair at the Half Yearly Meeting incident (and subsequent complaint ignored by the Company Secretary [Nick Eyre]) it is clear that the Secretariat assumes it has power over the elected members representing the membership – the owners. Hence the attitude: "The servants have become the masters."*

163 *In many organisations, intimate relationships are against their Codes of Conduct. Conflicts of interest could cause problems if, for example, a senior elected member was married to or the "lifestyle partner" of a member of staff. This does not seem to have been considered. The marriage of the Regional Chair to the Regional Area Committee Secretary was seen as a problem by the three SE Main Board Directors.*

164 *It may well be that some (perhaps many) may see that the Code revised in 2006 as an attempt to gag and control members even more than they were in 2003/4. Members in constant fear of breaching the Code will be vulnerable to threats or attack. Those who have experienced Autocratic Management styles know the lengths that some managers will go, to oust "difficult" employees. The same can apply to elected representatives. Under the Code, any reasonable member could quite easily transgress the Code, quite unintentionally. Most elected members are not lawyers, yet will be expected to operate within a framework which is a legal minefield. Legal terms have definitions and many lay people will not appreciate their nuances e.g. quotation vs. estimate (the former a fixed price, the latter not so); Tax Evasion vs. Tax Avoidance (the former illegal the latter legal). Many volunteers will not wish to operate in such a coercive system. Although each and every transgression of the code may not be punished at the time, it could be added to the file to try and build a case in the future. It is very important that this Code and subsequent rules are not simply nodded through and I urge members to conscientiously amend them accordingly, adding independent and robust support for elected members (see my article News ~9 Feb - 4 Mar 2008).   © Vic Parks*

165 Below, in italics, is the original wording of the 2006 Code. Analytical comments in bold.

166 *CG CODE OF CONDUCT FOR REGIONAL BOARD/AREA COMMITTEE MEMBERS**
the term 'committee member' is used to refer to both Regional Board members and Area Committee members.

167 *1.Introduction: This Code outlines appropriate conduct for elected members, and addresses both the requirements of office and their personal behaviour. The Code seeks to expand on or complement CG's Rules and Regional Regulations. A copy will be included in candidates' "Packs for the information of Members" who are considering seeking election to the CG's committees. It will be provided to all newly elected members and referred to in detail as part of the compulsory new committee members' induction training.*

168 *Members seeking election to the CG's committees will be required to sign a declaration on the nomination form to confirm that they will comply with the Code in all respects and that, in particular, they will support co-operative objectives.*

© Vic Parks 2014

169 **It is reasonable to request elected (or prospective) members to** *"support co-operative objectives,"* **but these are not defined and open to wide interpretation. Why are Principles and Values not used, instead of "objectives"? These underpin modern day Co-operation. Could it be that using principles and values instead could make "control" of members more difficult?**

170 *2.Qualifications for office: Committee members must continue to comply with the qualifications required to hold elected office throughout their period of tenure. The Committee Secretary must be advised by the member concerned of any changes in circumstance which disqualify the committee member from continuing in office. An example of this would be a committee member becoming an employee of the CG, given that the number of employees sitting on the CG's elected bodies is limited.* **Would the qualification also be the requirement to buy the minimum amount of CG goods and services?**

171 *3.Role and functions Committee members must:*
a. adhere to the CG's Rules and Regulations and support its objectives, in particular those of retaining co-operative status and developing a 'successful co-operative business'. **"Members must (support) Co-operative Status" and (in) "developing a successful co-operative business" are open to interpretation. Does the former mean, for example, not privatising the Co-op?**

b. (They must) act in the best interests of the CG at all times. **There are various subjective interpretations of this phrase. For example, an elected member could openly criticise the CG in public or press, which could be seen as breaching the Code. Although perhaps embarrassing to Management it could be in the long term best interests of the CG.**

c. (They must) contribute to the workings of their committee in order for it to fulfil its role and functions as defined in the CG's Rules and Regulations. **Is this aimed at the "the say nothing, do nothing" members?**

d. note that Regional Boards and Area Committees are subordinate to the Board of Directors.

e. recognise that their role is a collective one. They exercise collective decision making in the committee room which is recorded in the minutes. Outside the committee room an individual committee member has no more rights and privileges than any other member. **This needs clarification. Would a conscientious committee member be in breach by asking questions (e.g. of staff in a local store) which would assist his/her role?**

Note that the functions allotted to committees are not of a managerial nature.

172 *4. Confidentiality: Maintaining confidentiality is a shared responsibility between committee members and the CG. To facilitate this, the CG must indicate which matters are confidential in nature, with papers clearly marked as confidential where applicable. In circumstances where a discussion at a meeting is confidential, it will be the responsibility of the Chair or Officer present to highlight this explicitly to committee members. Confidential matters will include financial information relating to the CG's trading performance (that has not been placed in the public domain by the Society), development proposals, closure / disposal proposals, and papers from the Co-operative Group Board. In certain circumstances it will be necessary to*

remove reference to items of a confidential nature from minutes / reports which have a wider circulation.

173 *Disclosure of information that is deemed to be confidential will be regarded as a breach of this Code, irrespective of the consequence arising. Third parties to whom confidential matters must not be disclosed include customers, other members, elected members on lower tier committees or from other regions, employees of the Co-operative Group and its subsidiaries, competitors or the media. Although it is not possible to cover all eventualities, in general, members must assume that matters remain confidential until such time as the Society places the matter in the public domain.*

174 **This is the most highly contentious part of the Code. CG will deem what is and is not confidential and that means Management - giving them considerable power. I had much correspondence with the former Secretary, Nick Eyre on this very issue. At some stage it was suggested that written material (e.g. articles) for publication ought to be presented to the Secretariat. Clearly, it would be acting as censor with the likely possibility of stamping a "D Notice" on parts it dislikes. Arguably, confidentiality may be used by management to protect itself. For example, "Gagging" clauses for past and present employees can be used to cover up unethical, bad management practices. Criticism of management might be "struck out" on spurious grounds of breaking confidentiality. The Code comes very close to that** *"Although it is not possible to cover all eventualities, in general, members must assume that matters remain confidential until such time as the Society (Management) places the matter in the public domain."* **That would be a "catch all" paragraph. Members will not be able to discuss anything with anyone (other than within committees) without fear of transgressing the Code. Effectively, it is a "gagging" clause.**

175 **Debate is essential between co-operators for effective democracy, training and education. Blanket use of "confidentiality" stifles such debate. Committee members need to be clear as to what can and cannot be discussed outside the committee forum. Identifying guidelines is difficult, but a few suggestions:**

176 **Perhaps there needs to be a list of specific instances, which are absolutely confidential. Unless there is radical change, the specific area appears reasonable:** *Confidential matters will include financial information relating to the CG's trading performance (that has not been placed in the public domain by the Society), development proposals, closure / disposal proposals,*

177 **Issues that relate to the democratic structure and processes ought to be open and transparent. All the Group's members are part of the same family. The Co-operative News is about the only real and credible forum for debate of issues common to most members. The test would be that a breach is only when it would be of commercial advantage to a competitor or affect staff.**

178 **One problem is: - who decides what is confidential or in the Public Domain or, indeed, placed there? Perhaps there could be a lay, Confidential Advisory Panel (CAP) to help give guidance and ensure some Form of impartiality.**

179 **Some years ago I suggested, also, that no information passed to any member is to be treated as confidential unless each page of the copy of the document is specifically**

marked 'CONFIDENTIAL'. That is now the case but it is hampered by the Management deeming what is confidential, as it could mark any/or all documents "confidential" even when it is unnecessary. Thus, any document so marked could be referred to a suggested Confidential Advisory Panel by the committee/board as to whether it genuinely needs to be confidential.

180　From time to time, members disclose confidential information to me they ought not. Often, that is helpful and I respect their trust and confidentiality. To the letter of the Code, do I have duty to "shop" them? As a writer, confidentiality is essential with a duty to protect my sources.

181　What if a committee/Board discusses theft, fraud and corruption yet decides to hush it up and/or makes unethical decisions? Where does the conscientious elected member stand?

182　*5. Conflict of interests:*

183　*a.* **Personal Interests** *A member must regard themselves as having a personal interest in any matter if the decision on a matter might reasonably be regarded as affecting the wellbeing or financial position of the member, a relative or friend or any connected organisation, to a greater extent than that of other persons or organisations. A personal interest must be declared and recorded. The declaration does not automatically prevent a member from participating fully in debate and voting. For example, when considering applications for grant aid, funding or other support.*

184　*(i) If an elected member is a member of an organisation that is seeking support, the member must declare that interest but feel free to participate in any discussion about the proposal*

185　*(ii) If an elected member is actively involved in the governance of, or is employed by, an organisation that is seeking support, the member must declare that interest and refrain from participating in any discussion about the proposal. A member is not expected to know the personal interests of all their friends and relations, and is only expected to declare such an interest if they happen to be aware of it. The member must declare any personal interest at the beginning of the discussion of that particular item.*

186　*Conflict of Interest and Prejudicial Interest.* **It is clear that committee members must declare an interest, especially when dealing with financial matters that affect an organisation in which they are deeply involved or their "pet project." Probably, most Group committee members also belong to Group funded organisations: The Co-op Party, Woodcraft folk, Women's Guilds, and so on. Should this be declared on each and every occasion to comply with the Code?**

187　*(b) Prejudicial Interest: It is for the member to decide whether they have a 'prejudicial interest'.* **This is somewhat subjective and open to interpretation. To be safe, the member should declare an interest, no matter how tenuous the connection.**

188　*They must consider whether 'an ordinary member of the public, knowing all the relevant facts, would think that their personal interest was so significant that it would prejudice their decision on this matter'. A personal interest does not in itself require a member to cease to participate in the decision-making process. Only when that personal interest is also a prejudicial interest must a member consider withdrawing from the debate. If a member decides they have a prejudicial interest in a particular matter under discussion they must declare this and*

withdraw from the room. As well as absenting themselves from the discussion, they must not seek to influence a decision on that item; whether by attempting to sway the decision of any other members, or by exerting influence on an officer. This Code encompasses behaviour at all Society meetings within the
Region, including any sub-committees.

189 *(c) Exemptions from a need to declare an interest. There are a number of things which do not generally constitute a personal interest or a prejudicial interest which need to be declared. Examples are:*

190 *(i) where a member is 'dual hatted' and sits on more than one tier of Co-operative Group, Co-operatives UK, or Co-operative Party governance.* **This needs clarification as it seems to be a strange statement, as all these organisations are funded by Group. Why should they be exempted? Should not the opposite be the case?**

191 *(ii) where a member has been appointed or elected by a committee to act as its representative on another body, e.g., as a school governor*

192 *(iii) where a member receives legitimate out-of-pocket expenses from the Society.*

193 *The scale of the interest may nevertheless suggest that the interest must be declared and may be prejudicial, e.g. the Directors of the Society take part in most regional debates on national policy matters, but they withdraw for the Regional Board discussion on directors' fees.*

194 *(d) Recording of Interests It is sufficient, given the nature of the decisions and the organisations envisaged, that a declaration of interest be recorded in the Minutes of the appropriate committee. Currently a formal regional register of interests for committee members is not maintained by the Society.*

195 *(e) Declaring Gifts and Hospitality A member must declare any substantial gift or hospitality (the local council threshold is £25) but only if received as a result of their position as a committee member.*

196 *(f) Self-declaration In all cases considered above, members should seek guidance from the Area Committee Secretary or Regional Secretary regarding the appropriate action to be taken.*

197 *(g) Monitoring: It is not suggested that there be any formal mechanism for monitoring members' interests at regional or area level. It is believed that if members conduct themselves appropriately and seek officers' guidance when potential conflicts of interest arise, this will not be necessary.*

198 ***6. Committee meetings:*** *Committee members have a responsibility to attend meetings of their committee. When this is not possible they must submit an apology to the Committee Secretary in advance of the meeting. Absence from committee meetings without good reason established to the satisfaction of the committee (such as ill health, other co-operative business) is grounds for disqualification. A Group Board Director's absence, in particular, would be considered in light of other co-operative commitments they might have during a more extended period. Failure to attend at least half of the meetings in any financial year or absence from three consecutive meetings will result in the committee member being deemed to have resigned their*

position unless the grounds for absence are deemed to be satisfactory by the Regional Board/Area Committee. Committee members are expected to attend for the duration of the meeting. Members who persistently miss a significant proportion of the meeting will also be grounds for members to be reprimanded.

199 *7. **Personal conduct**: Committee members are required to adhere to the highest standards of conduct in the performance of their duties. In respect of their interaction with others, they are required to:*

200 *(a) Adhere to good practice in respect of the conduct of meetings and respect the views of their fellow elected members.*

201 *(b) Be mindful of conduct which could be deemed to be unfair or discriminatory.* **These are very important for effective committee work.**

202 *(c)Treat the Society's officers and other employees with respect and in accordance with the Society's policies for employees on bullying, harassment and discrimination as they may exist from time to time. Officers and employees in contact with elected members will be afforded the same rights of protection against bullying, harassment and discrimination as all other Co-operative Group employees.* **Again, one-sided statements and indicative of drafting bias in favour of the Secretariat? There is no reciprocal statement to protect elected members when there are instances of Institutional bullying, as in my case.**

203 *(d) Recognise that committees and management have a common purpose, i.e. the success of the CG and adopt a team approach.*

204 *(e) Committee members must conduct themselves in such a manner as to reflect positively on the CG. When attending external meetings or any other events to which they are delegated, it is important for committee members to be ambassadors for the CG, including where there is a social dimension to the event, such as dinners as receptions where alcohol is served.*

205 *"This Code encompasses behaviour at all Society meetings within the Region, including any sub- committees."* **This was strangely inserted under 5b, above, rather than in this section, 7. It seemed out of context to that section and perhaps better discussed under this section. Was this deliberate?**

206 **Defining good and bad "behaviour" is a minefield. What is "reasonable behaviour"? It is highly subjective. I have seen members censored by Chairs for passionately expressing their views. It is subjective and a question of definition and context. Many committee members in all walks of life can find themselves in a minority of one, taking a stance against the consensus. "Persistent" questioning, challenging Minutes, procedure and so on could be seen as "disruptive behaviour." Yet, freedom to criticise and question is essential for the elected person's role. There are many examples of undetected corruption and incompetence due to the fear of challenging ruling groups which operate under a dominating or Stalinist ethos.**

*8. **Whistleblowing:** The Society's existing process for whistleblowing for employees is applicable to elected members. Members can choose to highlight matters of concern in confidence to the designated officers appointed by the CG.* **The Whistle blowing process is now the same for employees and elected members (something I advocated years ago) using "designated officers appointed by the CG." The danger is that Management is in control: " ...** *the designated officers (staff?)* **(And in 15.e)** *"have absolute discretion to refer the matter to the most appropriate level in the CG for consideration"* **This gives Management/Secretariat considerable power over the situation. Company Secretary (Nick Eyre) offered his deputy (Moira Lees) as a mediator in my case. This was totally inappropriate as she was involved. He rejected my suggestion of an outside mediator (e.g. Alan Middleton). Potentially, being employees, CG Mediation staff could be subject to pressure from senior managers.**

207 **It is debatable as to whether elected members would be covered by the Public Interest Disclosure Act 1998. However, the Code does not explicitly describe the procedure or the criteria to "blow the whistle" and needs defining. For objectivity, especially where elected members wish to "blow the whistle on Management," should there be an independent body to refer to? From my experience, complaining to Senior Management probably bought about my demise, through facing spurious Secretariat allegations.**

208 *9. **Committee Chairs:** Training on chairing skills is a compulsory requirement for all meeting chairs (including members' meetings). The training includes how to deal with unacceptable behaviour from members as well as guidance of what might be reasonably considered to be bullying or harassment.* **This section was not in the 2003/4 Code. Was this because the Regional Secretary objected to me circulating a report around participating Chairs? It appears to be more evidence of her wish to control information, contributing to the CG apparent obsession with secrecy and "covering up negative information."**

209 *10. **Accountability:** Committee members are accountable to their electorate and must demonstrate this by attending members' meetings and other key events which provide opportunities to interface with their electorate in order to best represent their views.* **This is somewhat "hollow" when it appeared that the Regional Secretary and RB Chair tried to thwart my attempts to run forums for ordinary members, which was a good, tried and tested way of eliciting their views (See para 401 – 404).**

210 *11. **Financial matters:** Committees are responsible for monitoring and managing their annual budget, and acting responsibly at all times in the allocation of the Society's resources in line with national policy. Expenses are paid to delegates carrying out official duties as minuted by the committee or agreed with the appropriate officer. Committee members must ensure that levels of expenditure are within the Expenses Policy and that they obtain receipts for expenditure incurred. Fraudulent expense claims will be deemed to be a breach of the Code.*

211 *12. **Training and development:** Training is essential for committee members, both in respect of the effective performance of their current role, and to equip them for election to higher office. Committee members are required to adhere to the Society's policy in all respects.*

212 *13. **Visits to trading outlets:** Where committees wish to visit the premises of the Society in a formal capacity, as opposed to individuals in a personal capacity as consumers, the committee should liaise with the Area Committee Secretary to make the necessary*

arrangements.

213 ***14. Delegations:*** *All committee members must be prepared to be delegated to Society and wider Movement events. Those who are delegated are reminded that they are expected to:*

214 **I have considerable misgivings about the Delegate system, "Representative Democracy." (See 261)**

215 *(a)Report back to their committee at the meeting following the delegation*

216 *(b) Attend the event for its full duration and actively participate as appropriate.*

217 *(c) Act as delegates and representatives of the Society, not in an individual capacity.* **Under the current system, delegations decide how they are going to vote prior to the meeting. Therefore, any debate in a CG meeting is often academic and "hot air." In the interest of openness and fullness, it would be important for individuals (often representing the views of their committee) to have the right to put them to the meeting, clearly stating that they are personal views and contrary to the delegation's consensus? Apparently and currently, that is at the discretion of the delegation's Chair. To go further, delegates could make up their minds individually and vote accordingly. There could be a pre-meeting (e.g. SGM) discussion of Regional delegates but they may also know the views of their delegating committee and have listened to the delegates' from other regions, before they vote.**

218 *(d) Committees are encouraged to operate delegation rotas in order that all committee members have the opportunity to attend events bearing in mind that there may be an expectation at some events that office holders should be in attendance. Guidance can be sought from the Regional Secretary or Area Committee Secretary.* **The problem with this is that members not used to going to national events are disadvantaged by not knowing procedures and how things can be manipulated.**

219 ***15. Non-compliance with the Code of Conduct:*** *Non-compliance with the Code will result in action being taken as follows: - Where misconduct takes place, the Chair is authorised to take such action as may be immediately required, including the exclusion of the person concerned from a meeting.* **Under the Code, the meeting's Chair has the right to exclude a member. As this could be abused, perhaps there ought to be a vote of members present, on the exclusion with say a *70/30* majority or even higher. If the Chair's abuse was significant, then a vote of no confidence could ensue.**

220 *Where such misconduct is alleged, it will be open to the committee of which that person is a member to decide, by simple majority of those in attendance, to lay a formal charge of misconduct. In such instances, it will be the responsibility of the next tier of committee (or in the case of Regional Boards, a Panel consisting of the Society Secretary and two Directors, nominated by the Group Chair, from regions other than that concerned) to deal with it by:-*

221 *(a) notifying the member in writing of the charge/s, detailing the specific behaviour which is considered to be detrimental to the Society, and inviting and considering their response within a defined timescale;*

222 *(b) carrying out such investigation as the Regional Board (or Panel) consider appropriate;*

223 *(c) if the Regional Board (or Panel) do not consider the matter to have been resolved*

© Vic Parks 2014

satisfactorily through correspondence, convening a meeting and inviting such persons as they consider necessary (including the member against whom the allegation of misconduct has been made) to attend and address the Regional Board or sub-committee of that Regional Board set up for the purpose of investigating the complaint (or Panel) in person;

224 *(d) deciding, by simple majority of those present and voting, whether to uphold the charge of conduct detrimental to the Society;*

225 **If misconduct is alleged, "*... it will be open to the Committee of which that person is a member ... to lay a formal charge ... by a simple majority.*" Perhaps that also ought to be *70/30* or even higher. The next tier will deal with it, by correspondence or convening a Disciplinary Hearing, deciding again *"by simple majority ... (and) imposing such sanctions as shall be deemed appropriate."* Bearing in mind the jury system, perhaps it should be a much greater majority. There are likely to be carriages of injustice, due to bias, discrimination, misjudgement, bullying, incompetence, rivalry, personal dislikes, etc. To safeguard Natural Justice, an independent appeal procedure is imperative, as suggested at the start of this Critique.**

226 **It could be argued: if someone is found unjustly "guilty" of misconduct so what? The whole process of being unjustly accused is highly stressful and painful. In addition, the damage done to a person's reputation could be quite serious, especially within the Co-operative world. Other than suing for Defamation, elected members have no redress. Members on voluntary committees/bodies do sometimes sue for libellous articles in members' Newsletters and Magazines, but legal costs deter many. Added to that, any litigious process is highly stressful, especially if a member is alone without any legal support, unlike staff that may belong to a trade union. Two Co-operative values are: caring for others and social responsibility.**

227 **In the case of staff, Management have a duty of care. Should the CG have the same duty of care for elected members?**

228 **Should there be a rule with sanctions to guard against false, malicious or vexatious allegations designed to cause grief to others (opponents, disliked colleagues, rivalry, etc.)?**

229 *(e) Imposing such sanctions as shall be deemed appropriate. Such sanctions will range from the issuing of a written warning as to the member's future conduct and consequences, non-payment of fees and/or expenses/removal of discount card, to the removal of the member from office. In the event of misconduct being alleged, in respect of an Area Committee member, who sits on the Regional Board as its delegate, that member shall be excluded from consideration by the Regional Board of that matter. In the event of misconduct being alleged in respect of the Chair, the Vice Chair shall act as Chair for the purposes of this Code of Conduct. In circumstances where the matter concerns an alleged breach relating to the conduct of more than one member of a committee, the matter will automatically be escalated to the next tier of the committee structure. In circumstances where an issue is raised through the whistleblowing process, the designated officers have absolute discretion to refer the matter to the most appropriate level in the Society for consideration.*

End of Code of Conduct.

230 **Notification to Area Committees by Karen Froggatt**. *"Confidentiality issues - guidance notes."* **From the evidence of this document: it is clear that the Regional Secretary has considerable influence on confidentiality rules:** *"the Regional Board agreed that I should produce draft guidance notes on this subject."* **She continues:** *"In the event of the media contacting elected members, information which is (or may be) of a confidential nature should not be disclosed."* **This appears to be a gagging attempt.**

231 **In a lengthy document from the Company Secretary, headed "Confidentiality," (2006) he acknowledges that:** *"Within the Co-operative structure ... openness is fundamental"* *later adding:* *"... there will always be some grey areas in what may be complex situations. ...individuals are not prevented from raising their own and wider members' legitimate concerns."* **He suggests, of course, Regional Officials can give guidance to elected members but, due to the distrust between some elected members and the Secretariat, they may well feel that attempts will be made to gag them. Often heard is: "You can't say that because ...." Which is similar to "You can't do that because..." which is the usual excuse for deterring elected members putting forward proposals.**

232 **He continued:** *"As a Co-operative, it is at the heart of our principles that we are democratically controlled and balancing these imperatives against our principles is a difficult matter in practice. While there is not and should never be any attempt to stifle criticism and debate, (this should be) ... conducted through the appropriate channels and at the appropriate time..."* **Presumably, the appropriate channels being the Secretariat.**

233 **There is further evidence of the wish to control information, top down management and to treating Area Committee members as "serfs (see para 262)":** *"Whilst it is understandable that Regional Board members may wish to share information with Area Committees or the general membership at the earliest opportunity, this creates a tension with the legal/commercial dynamics and it is not always acceptable to do so. This often may be a judgement call and it is sometimes hard to be definitive in a given case."* *14/7/06*

234 **These quotations show that "confidentiality" clashes with Co-operative principles of honesty and openness. It is a minefield and elected members could easily fall foul of somewhat subjective judgements as to what is confidential or not. Elected members throughout the national organisation have common issues that affect them all. Sharing information is essential. Unfortunately, the Secretariat appears to want to rigidly control information, adopting "trickle down" or "drip, drip" methods.**

235 **One of the most important organs for sharing ideas and experience, nationally, is the Co-operative News, and its independence is very important. Unfortunately, it is subject to CG funding, directly or indirectly and the editorial staff are under pressure not to be overly critical. Thus, prior to the current debacle, there was a view that the Co-op News was cynically called "The CG News." At the time, I amended that of the "CG GOOD News." But, in the current situation the "good news" is hard to find.**

FREE SPEECH

The Bedrock of Co-op Democracy; But also Co-operative Group Hypocrisy?

236 **FREE SPEECH** is essential for democracy and democracy is at the heart of a Co-operative or Mutual. Without the organisation being truly democratic, it cannot call itself a Co-operative or mutual. I have fought many years in the CG emphasising the importance of democracy and free speech, writing many articles on these themes. Below is an edited version of my draft, published as an article in 2003. The issues covered are somewhat timeless as they are equally pertinent today, as then. Indeed, as far as free speech and democracy is concerned, the situation in CG is far worse, eleven years on.

237 Although the CG Secretariat hypocritically espouses Co-operative Principles, there is little doubt that it tries to stifle free speech. It wishes to control what goes into the Public Domain, as "it knows best." We live in an age of "spin" where an articulate representative ("The Voice") of an organisation (e.g. a utility) tries to convince the public that "everything is fine," even when the evidence is to the contrary. Although the Secretariat may believe that it is right to defend the CG, taken to extremities it stifles debate and deters elected representatives holding management to account, their fundamental role and duty.

238 There needs to be a balance of co-operative principles of honesty and openness verses the problem of breaching confidentiality that may, for example, assist a competitor.
……………………………………………………..

239 **CO-OPERATIVE DEMOCRACY AND ACCOUNTABILITY** By Vic Parks 2003

240 Draft of an article published 12 April 2003 Entitled: Why Free Speech is the Bedrock of Co-op Democracy"

241 *Free speech is the bedrock of democracy; and one of the central principles of Co-operation is "democracy." Pauline Green reinforces this view: "the principles of international co-operation, is very clear in terms of democracy and participation …"*

242 *Exchanging differing points of view or criticism is the lifeblood of the Co-operative Cause. This is why some co-operators are becoming concerned. Others, who are often in positions of significant "economic power and influence," appear to want to "gag" the Co-op News. Geoffrey Whitely (former editor) identifies "working off personal grudges" and "senior executives who do not, on the whole, welcome debate" as being some explanations for this (News, 1:3:2003). Barbara Rogers put it more bluntly two weeks previously: "The suppressed fury of some senior executives and others who have read in it something they didn't like (perhaps years ago!)." As I have previously argued, the News must retain its independent editorial freedom (News 25:5:2002),*

243 *It is nice to live in a "cosy consensus." Many years ago, someone said to me: "It's the easiest thing in the world to be a conservative." By that, he meant, go along with the status quo. UK citizens ought to feel privileged that they live in their country. Rights, freedoms, standard of living and so on are invariably taken-for-granted. Many are complacent about contemporary society, as if its current norms and values are "in stone." Yet history shows that the future is fragile and uncertain.*

244 *What "is" today has been hard fought for by many previous generations, not only in physical wars but also in fighting for their beliefs. Racism, sexism, genderism, ageism and many other "isms" are battles that have been won or progressed by the courage of individuals or small minorities. At the start of their battles, they are often ridiculed and ostracised for their beliefs. Invariably, it is a lonely road. Fighting for principles and causes means "putting your head above the parapet." When one does (as I did with trying to save Stanford Hall for future co-operators, News, 5:5: 2001), one gets shot at as one is challenging the "leaders." Criticism, especially of our "leaders," is necessary for any healthy organisation. However, it is the critic's motives that matter. Is the critic being constructive or deliberately destructive? Is his/her opposition out of belief or dislike of an individual?*

245 *I am an educationalist and a "philosopher." Perhaps the latter sounds a bit pompous, but the point is that I believe strongly in philosophical debate. Alternative opinions and views are essential for a healthy Co-operative Movement, or any organisation. However, the key element in a democracy is respecting others' right to hold different views to our own. It is most important that our personal dislike for someone must not turn into personal vendettas, or the undermining and destruction of someone through Machiavellian tactics. It is the issues and arguments that matter. Unfortunately, there are those who become irrational, vindictive enemies of others who take a different point of view. In my view, they are not true democrats. Fortunately, in the UK, we are not killed for our beliefs, if they are anti-establishment or against the status quo. Having stated this, some might argue that there are others ways of "getting" or "assassinating" intellectual opponents.*

246 *Len Burch is a decent and dedicated long-term co-operator. A former lecturer at the Co-operative College, his letter in the News (8:2:2003) was expressing a growing concern about Co-operative Education. The loss of Stanford Hall meant the loss of a symbol of stability and an environment conducive to learning, which I expressed in my News article 4:8:2001. Indeed, eighteen months later, Alistair Graham's letter 29:3:03, lamenting the loss of Stanford Hall, reinforced my arguments. In-house, regional training has a major flaw, as it is in danger of becoming incestuous and sterile. A rich source of Co-operative Education was meeting co-operators from other parts of the country and, indeed, the World. Sharing experience, knowledge and ideas, in a residential setting (which was considered to be our own), is an important part of the learning process.*

247 *The Scottish Co-op Party used to run a Summer School at St Andrews University. I had a very positive attitude to the event. When I first went there in 1999, I was very disillusioned with local politics. I had suffered from extreme Machiavellianism after becoming more active in the Labour Party in the mid-90s when I became CLP Secretary and Political Education Officer. After about four years in active local politics, I had become disillusioned with my local Constituency Labour Party and was on the point of dropping out. Excesses of cliques, nepotism, individual power, Machiavellian strategies and so on, cause much damage to party structures and the morale of the ordinary active membership. Such practices drive many good, talented people away and reinforce the populous attitude: "They are only in it for themselves."*

248 *However, the St Andrews Co-op Summer School gave me an understanding that politics and political organisations could be DIFFERENT. The warmth, friendliness and supportiveness probably kept me involved in the political scene.*

249 *For all of us in the Co-operative Movement, we must respect each other's opinions and views. Some say that there is an "Awkward Squad" whose members are only interested in "opposing everything." Even they need to be accommodated since they may make valid arguments. In the*

Co-operative Movement (Co-op Group, Co-op Party), we need to demonstrate that politics and other democratic organisations can be different. Intolerance is the World's biggest enemy. We need to question peoples' motives when they offer criticism or opposing views. Are they being constructive or irrationally destructive? We also need to be wary of Machiavellianism that can be a destructive force in politics and organisations.

250 *Praise is a rare commodity, especially when one's head is above the parapet. The then organisers Joe Hill and Pat Watters, et al, organised and ran the Scottish Summer School, which many saw as very successful. In part this was due to their hard work, but the co-operation and motivation of the course participants was essential. As a fellow trainer and educationalist, my praise (from a contemporary) ought to carry considerable weight.*

251 *Co-operation is about honesty, openness and democracy. We need to ensure honest and open debate in the "seeking of truth" and the search for the "right path."*

252 *There is a growing feeling that "Control Freakery" is emerging in the drive to ensure an influential Co-operative voice. There appears to be tensions between CG organisational employees and elected members; and Co-operative ideologues and "businesslogues." The former may be seen as the idealists rooted in the Founders Co-operative principles. The latter may be seen as more concerned about Co-operative economic success. The truth is, one needs the other and, in an "ideal world," they are one of the same. Another growing concern is whether democracy, through elected members on committees, etc., is getting squeezed out. Voices from the grass troops need to be heard and, when rational, acted upon by our "leaders." We, who exist on the lower tiers, need to praise the courage of the Co-op News' editor. In the current uncertain climate, I feel sure that he has considerable pressure from above (from the CG). Yet he has to ensure that the voices of those without power and influence can be heard. After all, ordinary members are the Co-operative Movement and, therefore, its "Guardians" for future generations."*

253 *There is a real danger that the "thrusters," who have a vision of a better Co-operative World, may attempt to squash those who might impede their progress towards their aims. It appears that our leaders need to be less sensitive and defensive about criticism. When one becomes a "leader," one must expect to be questioned. Their heads are above the parapet. If the democracy doesn't work, The Co-op might just as well become another PLC and forget Co-operative Principles and Values. © Vic Parks 2003.*

254 The Scottish Co-op Party Summer School (then Fest), ran along discussion groups and plenary feedback lines which emphasised the importance of sharing experience, ideas, views, expertise, etc. at a national level. Although the "formal" sessions were important, because it was residential, much was to be shared over meals, drinks and so on. Although somewhat less tangible in terms of achieving learning objectives, it was SO important to meet others from different parts of the UK from, perhaps, different cultures. Bonds were built and there was a sense of shared identity. When I was in the Merchant Navy, meeting people from other parts of the UK enriched me through empathy, comradeship, understanding of others and their cultures.

255 The Co-op News is the main organ for information, analysis and discussion by active Co-operators. As it is important for the Co-operative Movement, editorial freedom is vital to provide balance. However, because the CG funds it directly or indirectly - through sales of the newspaper – the CG management may, implicitly or explicitly, apply pressure upon the editorial staff. There needs to be a way of independently funding the newspaper.

256 Another forum for discussion is perhaps through a debating web site where views and information can be exchanged, but the CG "KGB" would probably want to control free flow discussion. Perhaps, if there had been wider discussion of CG issues, especially the takeovers, perhaps the CG disaster would not have happened. I understand, recently, that elected members have been "asked" not to write to the Co-operative News. Is this yet another example of suppressing information?

19 FEB – 4 MAR 2008

Right of free speech needs to be at heart of review

By Vic Parks

THE UK Co-operative Movement is at a crossroads beside a pillar at a most significant time in its history.

It remains to be seen whether the pillar is a cold block of inert stone perpetuating the current system, even in a revised form, or one that contains collective co-operative knowledge, experience, understanding and wisdom.

My fervent hope is that the current review process becomes a watershed and a giant leap forward for the Movement and co-operatively minded individuals in an increasingly volatile political, economic and social environment.

In my view, the fundamental issue to be addressed by the review group is the current vulnerability and weak position of elected lay representatives in co-operatives and mutuals.

The Co-operative Group states that it owns 85 per cent of UK co-operative retail. This gives it enormous power within the Movement and there is little doubt that many organisations are resisting the temptation to be critical of the Group for fear of losing favour and financial support.

In such a climate, open and analytical debate (a prerequisite for effective democracy) is being crushed.

Since the merger of the Group and United, enormous power is concentrated within a very small group of people and, in my view, a 'control freak culture' has been established within management and senior lay committees and boards. Added to that is the serious problem where (in simplistic terms) the "servants have become the masters".

A former Congress President and Lincoln Co-op President Alan Middleton wrote in the News of August 23rd 2005: "It is a sad day when a professional officer chooses to break with a 134-year-old convention that paid officials do not engage in a personal attack on democratically elected lay directors. The Movement is already over-dominated by paid officers, employees of the Movement, who will not rest until the voice of the lay member has been completely silenced."

And the same year, Co-op Party NEC member Geraint

Lay representatives are fundamentally on their own

Day commented: "In a number of societies there have been instances of bullying behaviour, defamation, vindictiveness or an unwillingness to accept collective responsibility. The result can be that some colleagues might fear to participate at all. Maybe these situations contribute to the cases where directors do not contribute to meetings for fear of being bullied, intimidated or embarrassed."

I too have experienced similar problems. I believe passionately in Co-op ideals — the Movement's values and principles. In an uncertain and troubled world, co-operation is a paradigm which may offer hope for future generations.

However in my ten years active experience within the Co-operative Movement, I have met a great deal of hypocrisy and injustice in terms of two of our principles/values: democracy (including free speech) and caring for others.

Within the Co-operative Group, there is undoubted pressure from the Secretariat to silence or marginalise dissenting voices and, as stated earlier, there is considerable fear pervading the Movement that opinions that might "rock the boat" could damage the position of individuals and organisations with vested interests.

Unfortunately, when a lay member is disciplined for speaking out or breaking so-called 'confidentiality' rules there is no independent appeal process. In similar circumstances, employees have trade union support plus the protection of employment law, legal advice and support. Lay representatives do not and are, fundamentally, on their own.

As illustrated by Enron and, perhaps, Northern Rock it is essential that dissenting voices can be heard.

Members on committees and boards are sometimes accused of being "nodding donkeys". In theory, they control the business on behalf of the membership that elects them but — in practice — senior management and the Secretariat dominate and have all the power.

The prevailing attitude is that management "knows best" and will not tolerate criticism or disagreement. The Group Constitutional Review needs to address the weakness, helplessness and vulnerability of elected lay representatives.

There needs to be:

1. An independent body for members to complain to;
2. An independent appeals tribunal;
3. A statutory right for elected lay members to belong to a trade union (or its equivalent) to give independent support. Membership fees to be paid for by the co-op they represent;
4. Whistle blowing rights, similar to those afforded to staff.

Legislation

There is another possibility — through legislation. Currently, HM Treasury has a consultation process into co-operatives and mutuals and a working party has been set up to help frame legislation.

Under Section 2.18/2.20 Corporate Governance and Accountability, it could incorporate statutory rights for elected lay members, using the essence of the above proposals.

For a co-operative to function properly, it needs to be firmly grounded in its ethical principles. Co-operation is more that just a "business".

It is a set of principles and values to act as a beacon for future generations living in a world where there is potential for enormous social upheaval, unrest and anarchy.

True co-operation is an alternative to autocratic, totalitarian states. But to be effective the right of free speech and criticism needs to be rigorously upheld with lay representatives properly supported, protected and free from fear of speaking out.

Being inheritors of the co-operative vision, the current elected representatives are the "guardians" with an obligation to uphold what the founders fought for and established.

One co-operator remarked to me recently: "There's an elephant in the room, but no one is talking about it."

If co-operators want to begin to reverse the anti-democratic tide, they must make a stand. The task for the Review Group is to guarantee openness, real democratic control and protection for elected lay members through a sympathetic trade union. Hopefully, it's not too much to ask for.

• Vic Parks is a member of the Co-operative Group's Surrey & Berkshire Area Committee, but writes in a personal capacity.

19

Why free speech is the bedrock of Co-op democracy

RAUL LIBERTAD WALDEZ'S letter in the *News*, 29th March states that *Postbag* letters are full of "bitter, petty personal conflicts" and "the same few people each week exchange their bile."

Well, that's one interpretation! Free speech is the bedrock of democracy; and one of the central principles of co-operation is democracy. Pauline Green reinforces this view in her letter alongside Raul's: "The principles of international co-operation, are very clear in terms of democracy and participation...".

It may be different in Chile, but exchanging differing points of view or criticism is the lifeblood of the co-operative cause. This is why some co-operators are becoming concerned. Others, often in positions of economic power and influence, seem to want to gag the *News*, as former Editor Geoffrey Whiteley and Co-operative Press director Barbara Rogers have stated in the past.

As I have previously argued that the *News* must retain its independent editorial freedom (*News*, 25th May, 2002), I will not recycle those arguments here.

Many years ago, someone said to me: "It's the easiest thing in the world to be a conservative." By that, he meant to go along with the *status quo*. UK citizens ought to feel privileged that they live in their country. Rights, freedoms, standard of living and so on are taken for granted. Many are complacent about contemporary society, as if its current norms and values are in stone. Yet history shows the future is fragile and uncertain.

What is today has been hard fought for by many previous generations, not only in wars but in fighting for their beliefs. Racism, sexism, ageism and other "isms" are battles that have been won or progressed by the courage of individuals or minorities.

At the start of their battles, they are often ridiculed and ostracised for their beliefs. Invariably, it is a lonely road. Fighting for principles means putting your head above the parapet. When you do that (as I did a couple of years ago when trying to save Stanford Hall) you get shot at as one who is challenging the leaders.

Criticism, especially of our "leaders", is necessary for any healthy organisation. However, it is the critics' motives that matter. Are they being constructive or deliberately destructive? Is their opposition out of belief or dislike of an individual?

I am an educationalist and a "philosopher". Perhaps the latter sounds a bit pompous, but I believe strongly in philosophical debate. Alternative opinions and views are essential for a healthy Movement, or any organisation.

However, the key element in a democracy is respecting others' right to hold different views to our own. It is important that our personal dislike for someone should not turn into personal vendetta, or the undermining and destruction of someone through Machiavellian tactics. It is the issues and arguments that matter.

Irrational

Unfortunately, there are some who become irrational, vindictive enemies of those who take a different point of view. In my view, they are not true democrats. Fortunately, in the UK, we are not killed for our beliefs if they are anti-establishment or against the *status quo*.

A recent example of a debate where the rank and file appear to be out of step with the leadership came in the correspondence to the News relating to the future of co-operative education. In my view, the current emphasis on in-house, regional training has a major flaw, in that it is in danger of becoming incestuous and sterile. A rich source of co-operative education used to be in meeting co-operators from other parts of the country and, as in Raul's case, the world.

Sharing experience, knowledge and ideas, in a residential setting is an important part of the learning process. Raul's positive experience of the Scottish Co-op Party's Summer School at St Andrews underlines this.

The concern, whether real or imagined, is that the Co-operative College is going to be lost in cyberspace, with the liquid assets of the Stanford Hall sale eventually trickling down the drain .

Raul praises the class of people he met at the Co-op Party Summer School and suggests that these people should write to the *News*. Well, I'm one of them! I attended in 1999 and 2001 and, like Raul, have a positive attitude to the event.

CO-OP activist and educationalist VIC PARKS has been perusing recent letters in the *News* *Postbag* pages and concludes that if free speech is to be stifled because of commercial and other pressures, the UK Co-op might as well become just another PLC.

STANFORD HALL... Still missed by many co-operators.

upon, I cannot say.

When I first went there, I was disillusioned with local politics. I had suffered from Machiavellianism after becoming active in the Labour Party in the mid-1990s when I became CLP Secretary and Political Education Officer. The report to my Surrey and Berkshire Area Committee sums up my feelings at the time:

My overarching positive gain from the 1999 Co-op Summer School was an understanding that politics and political organisations could be DIFFERENT. The warmth, friendliness and support probably kept me involved in the political scene.

After about four years in local politics, I became disillusioned with my local constituency Labour Party. Cliques, nepotism, individual power, Machiavellian strategies and so on cause damage to party structures and the morale of the ordinary members. Such practices drive many talented people away and reinforce the populous attitude: "They are only in it for themselves".

All of us in the Co-operative Movement must respect each other's opinions. Some say that there is an awkward squad whose members are only interested in opposing everything, but even they need to be accommodated since they may make valid arguments. In the Co-operative Movement we need to demonstrate that politics and other democratic organisations can be different.

Intolerance is the world's biggest enemy. We need to question peoples' motives when they offer criticism or opposing views. Are they being constructive or irrationally destructive? We also need to be wary of Machiavellianism that can be a destructive force.

Praise is a rare commodity, especially when one's head is above the parapet, but let's give it when it deserved.

Joe Hill and Pat Watters *et al*, organise and run the Scottish Summer School. Its success is due to their hard

considerable weight. My view is that this event is excellent and well worth the cost to send co-operators.

Let's also give praise to Pauline Green and her crew, whose strength of character is a powerful voice and driving force. Her political pedigree is a strength for the Movement. She is advancing the cause of co-operation and driving important strategies to encourage and broaden the co-operative community in its various forms.

Honesty

However, co-operation is also about honesty, openness and democracy. We need to ensure honest and open debate in the seeking of truth and the search for the right path.

There is a growing feeling that control freakery is emerging in the drive to ensure an influential co-operative voice. There appear to be tensions between Co-op employees and elected members; and Co-op ideologues and "businesslogues".

The former may be seen as the idealists rooted in the founders' co-operative principles. The latter may be seen as more concerned about economic success. The truth is, one needs the other and in an ideal world they are one and the same.

Another growing concern is whether democracy, through elected members on committees, etc, is getting squeezed out. Voices from the grass-roots need to be heard and, when rational, acted upon by our leaders.

We, who exist on the lower tiers, need to support the freedom of opinion concept that permeates the *News*. The voice of those without power and influence deserve to be heard – after all, ordinary members are the Movement and, therefore its guardians for future generations.

If the democracy doesn't work, the Co-op might just as well become another Plc and forget co-operative principles

48

6

news Features

May 25, 2002

COMMENT

Co-operative News No. 4318
Holyoake House, Hanover Street,
Manchester M60 0AS
Tel: 0161 214 0870 Fax No. 0161 214 0878

Co-operative Group makes right

GIVEN the Co-operative Group's crucial, not to say dominant, role in the UK Co-operative Movement, there has been a good deal of interest in the search to find a successor to Sir Graham Melmoth, who plans to retire at the end of September just a few months before his 65th birthday next March.

Even before the official selection procedure started, the Sunday Mirror was first out of the traps with the "news" that "under-fire Camelot boss Dianne Thompson has been lined up to take over as Chief Executive of the Co-op." Later, according to a report in *The Independent* newspaper, the favourite was said to be the Co-operative Group's own Retail Controller, Malcolm Hepworth.

Other names linked in the national press with the prestigious position included Mervyn Pedelty, Chief Executive of the highly-successful Co-operative Bank and, of course, Martin Beaumont, whose fine work as Chief Executive of United Co-op has clearly been noted well outside the confines of United's Stoke-on-Trent headquarters.

Apart from Mr Beaumont, who last week emerged as the winner of this fascinating contest, we have no way of knowing whether any of the above named individuals were ever serious candidates or even whether they were candidates at all. The same applies to the former Co-op executive and three other "outsiders" who Co-op Movement "insiders" say were short-listed for the position.

The speculation and guessing games may not be welcome, but they are an integral part of any high-profile selection process. Now that the issue has been resolved, it is important that the new incumbent gets the full backing and support of not only staff and colleagues at the Co-operative Group but people with the good of co-operation at heart throughout the land.

Irrespective of who did or who did not apply to succeed Sir Graham Melmoth in September, Martin Beaumont looks the perfect choice. His track record at United speaks for itself; he has a thorough knowledge of the Co-op Movement and of the workings of the Co-operative Group. He is enough of an "outsider" to bring a new and fresh approach to the Co-op Group's multi-million pound businesses and he is enough of an "insider" not to need a long time to find his feet in his new role.

In short, he is the right man at the right time. We wish him well.

Robert Owen Museum

A unique museum telling the remarkable story of the Welshman who inspired the Co-operative Movement. Admission free. Groups welcome by appointment.

Mon - Fri 9.30am - noon and 2 - 3.30pm
Sat 9.30 - 11.30am

The Cross, Broad Street, Newtown SY16 2BB
Tel: 01686 626345

PLEA TO THE PRESS REVIEW BOARD

An independent News is vital for the Movement

By VIC PARKS

SHARING ideas and views is the lifeblood of any organisation. A cosy, convergent, consensus usually leads to stagnation and decline. For the Co-operative Movement, steeped in tradition and founded upon ideological principles, debate is essential for survival.

As society and the commercial world changes in terms of norms, values and structures, the Co-operative Movement needs to respond.

As times change, its beliefs and values will either be under attack or in fashion, depending upon the prevailing climate. Thus it is essential for the Co- operative Movement to use its values and principles as an anchor while the co-operative ship responds to climatic changes in the commercial world. It needs to swing on the metaphorical anchor of its principles and values. Without these, it is no better than corporate capitalism that exploits workers and customers to maximise profit.

Opportunities

The *Co-operative News* should be an important medium for the exchange of views and ideas to help the wider Co-operative Movement to respond to change. With tightening budgets and more centralised control in co-operative administration and education, there are going to be fewer opportunities for ordinary activists to express and exchange views.

From my limited experience of Congress and Education Conventions, I found these somewhat sterile, stage-managed and sanitised events. Often, I went away with the feeling 'Where's the debate?'. At last November's Special Congress in Manchester, the Chair was almost pleading for speakers to oppose motions! Most went through more or less on the nod.

At Education Convention, one delegate agonised over whether he should speak against a motion because he felt his hands were tied by his organisation's mandated view. Is this healthy for democracy and, indeed, the wider Movement? Sharing views, beliefs and attitudes is crucial for educational processes.

I sense that the political wing of the Co-operative Movement (the Co-operative Party) is viewed by some influential members with suspicion. Or, perhaps, seen as an irrelevant and an unnecessary drain on resources for a relatively small return. If this is the case, this is a very narrow view.

Directly or indirectly, politics touches all aspects of our lives: the air we breathe, the countryside we walk in, the media we watch and listen to, how we relate to others, our sex lives, our work places and so on. Healthy and informed debate is the cornerstone of democracy. The communications media, in its various forms, is an essential part of the process.

Commercial success IS important since it is used as a measure of whether co-operative beliefs and values will work in practice. Long-term, empirical evidence of success helps strengthen our arguments and ward off our opponents. However, the Co-operative Movement is not just about commercial success. It is a set of ideals and an ideology that signposts the way to a better society, whether nationally, internationally or even just local communities.

In many ways, the current generation of activists, whether volunteers or employees, are the guardians of the vision of the founding co-operators. It is for us to keep it alive through good and bad times.

One of our contemporary voices is the *Co-operative News*, not just outside the Movement, but within. It must have editorial independence from the co-operative 'executive', in its various formats.

What do we want the *Co-operative News* to be? If it becomes a bland propaganda sheet highlighting all the positives, while ignoring the unsavoury aspect of co- operation, it will soon spiral into decline. Few will bother to read it or give its content any true validity. A balanced but rigorous *Co-operative News* should be inspirational and a check on the excesses of the co-operative 'elite'.

For me, as a member of an Area Committee and Regional Values and Principles Committee and a public advocate of Co-operative ideology, the headlines of the *Co-operative News* (27th April 2002) bring embarrassing shame upon us all. It is ammunition to our opponents.

As honesty and openness are two of our fundamental principles, it would be tempting for an editor to ignore unsavoury headlines. However, they are an important reminder that people are human, no matter how elevated and trusted they become. Thus, highlighting prominent employees' dishonesty, though perhaps damaging, is of service to the Co-operative Movement.

Headlines such as these underline the importance of committee members' inquisitorial role and give comfort and justification when they ask those awkward questions of management and the co-operative elite.

Safety

A publication that airs minority views has the function of being a safety valve. I used to be a long-term trustee of a small national charity. Many years ago I suggested a 'Gripes' publication to go alongside its bland, positive internal publication. I could see a growing dissension, frustration and disconnection within the organisation. I felt that airing of views would help heal some of the rifts. Unfortunately, the ruling clique sidelined the idea, even though the trustees passed it.

Several years later, the in-fighting led to a libel action. This was costly not only in monetary terms but especially, in the time wasted at trustees' meetings discussing legal matters. The in-fighting continues and the charity could be seen as a lame duck.

In my view, under the current editorial team and trustees, the *Co-operative News* provides a good balance. It liberally promotes co-operative retail activities while at the same time providing a forum for debate, especially by the grass-roots membership, of co-operative issues. It is educational and informative.

Whatever the current Co-op Press Review's conclusions will be, if the issue comes up at Congress, delegates need to be very cautious about handing over control of the *Co-operative News* to small, vested interests.

Responsible editorial independence is vital to ensure the continuation of a healthy, vibrant co-operative publication rooted in co-operative values and principles of honesty and openness.

• **Vic Parks is a training and education services consultant. He stood as Labour/Co-op candidate for Reigate and Redhill in the recent local council elections.**

© Vic Parks 2014

GOVERNANCE

UNdemocratic Structures – The Democratic Deficit.

257 **DEMOCRACY** allegedly makes co-operatives and mutuals different from PLCs. Theoretically; the "business" is "owned and controlled by its members." Janet Cato pointed out that problems arise when Co-ops become too big (Society for Co-operative Studies Conference 2010) – i.e. "small is beautiful." In small organisations, such as worker co-ops, it is relatively easy to communicate with all the members and involve them directly in decision making. However, with the representative democratic model, as in the CG, the major criticism of many activists is that the hierarchy becomes remote from the grassroots membership. Thus, The Main and Regional Boards made decisions which, probably, the majority of the membership disapproved. At the time of the last Constitutional Review, Dame Pauline Green (then CEO of Co-operative UK) argued in an article (Co-op News 22 Jan 2008) that there should be some form of One Member One Vote (OMOV), especially for Main/Regional Directors. This is little different from Building societies. On-line voting, etc. facilitates easy and economic voting. However, as Pauline pointed out: *"(will the Review) be a co-operative fudge put together to defend vested interests and appease local sentiment?"* This proved to be the case. In a draft article with the working title of "Constitutional Review – Self Interest Rules OK?" I also predicted the Review's outcome: it changed little in terms of Governance.

258 **BACKGROUND - CO-OPERATIVE GROUP STRUCTURE**

259 Unique to Co-operatives, Shareholders (members) should have one vote, even if they have more than one share. This underlines the principle of the business being **owned and run by its members** through, in theory, elected members i.e. **Indirect Democracy.** The Group structure is Area Committees (approximately 12 members) who elect Regional Board (15) members. Regions elect Main Board (21) members (2 in the South East). However, there is a number of "Corporate representatives" who are mainly Chief Executives of independent Retail Co-operatives. A hierarchy of employees (staff, who can also be members) undertake the day-to-day running. Idealistically, the elected members and staff work co-operatively for common goals but in the CG, the elected members are little more than a fig leaf for democracy. Metaphorically, "the servants have become the masters." The deep concern about the democracy can be found within its Letters pages of the Co-operative News, below.

260 **INDIRECT DEMOCRACY – THE DELEGATE SYSTEM**

261 I have considerable misgivings about the Delegate system, "Representative Democracy." **(See 217 - 218**) Under the current system, delegations decide how they are going to vote prior to the meeting. Therefore, any debate in a CG meeting is often academic and "hot air." In the interest of openness and fullness, would it not be more democratic for individuals (often representing the views of their committee) to have the right to put them to the meeting, clearly stating that they are personal views and contrary to the delegation's consensus? Apparently, and currently, that is at the discretion of the delegation's Chair. To go further, delegates could make up their minds individually and vote accordingly i.e. without a delegation consensus? There could be a pre-meeting (e.g. SGM) discussion by Regional delegates. However, before voting, they would have the benefit of the views of delegates from other regions and their delegating committee.

262 **The DEMOCRATIC DEFICIT** is the iceberg that has dominated the CG agenda for many years. Hundreds, if not thousands, of letters and articles have been sent to the Co-op News solely on this issue by many Co-op activists and past/current members on committees. Generally, grassroots

members feel utterly disenfranchised, helpless and unable to change things or influence policy. Motions from members put to general meetings, if passed, go into a "black hole" or just side-lined, if the ruling groups (especially the Secretariat) do not want them. Many elected members join with enthusiasm and zeal, yet quickly become disillusioned as they soon learn that they can make little difference: *"In relation to the current Quinquennial Review, it is obvious to me that democracy s fast vanishing, The CG Board ignores the views of area committee and regional boards and, as a consequence, we are 'ruled' from 'above,' like serfs..." Robin Martaikes 8 – 22 Aug 2006.* This is just one representative example. Eventually they leave. Further illustrations of frustration felt by many activists are as follows:

263 *"Individual members of the CG have never, to my knowledge, been consulted about anything. The rigidly structured area meetings that might provide them with an opportunity to influence events do nothing of the sort. It is hardly surprising that few members show an interest in the society's affairs. This massive democratic deficit is the CG'Ss core problem." Denis Hayes News 3-17 Oct 2006*

264 *"As to democratic control, it is hard to see how the CG can truly be considered a primary cooperative since the individual members do not vote for Board members, do not have a vote on the annual report and accounts, and cannot attend the AGM." MD Mathieson. News 20 Sep - 4 Oct 2005*

265 Historically, there has been conflict and a tussle between **elected members and management/Secretariat,** since the former is supposed to hold the latter to account. Over the years, the democracy has been eroded to such an extent that it is very weak and that process has been at least influenced or, at worst, contrived by the Management/Secretariat, as shown:

266 *"Milking the cash cow while destroying the democratic structure of our (Co-operative) Movement by stealth appears to be the tactic of the present Co-op Group hierarchy" Vic Parks is absolutely right in his recent article headlined "CG cuts are damaging the fabric of our Movement." My only criticism is that he appears to seriously underestimate the threat ... I feel that our democratic birth right and institution are once again under attack-only this time from within .... The present regional board system is anti-democratic and simply does not work.... Let the Co-operative Group hierarchy have their excessive pay and pension if you must, but don't let them steal your co-operative democracy. " Philip Rapier Co-op News 23 Aug - 6 Sep 2005*

267 *" ... many Area Committee members are incensed at the perceived cynicism of the Board in deferring the Quinquennial Review, only to introduce it shortly afterwards and without any prior consultation. Project Exchequer, a management led project that purports to make savings but in reality are cuts; a project that takes no account of the Co-operative Difference; and a project that is more concerned with implementing decisions already taken by the CG Board rather than involving members in reaching and taking ownership of those decisions. " Ron Hunter (former Regional Secretary) Co-op News 23 Aug- 6 Sept 2005*

268 *"Recent letters have expressed the view that the democratic structure of the CG is under threat, I agree. I am disappointed that savage cuts have been imposed upon committees in a cavalier and undemocratic manner, without taking into account the fact that ordinary members, rather than management, own the society and should have been fully involved in the cut back debate, rather than being presented with a fait accompli." Robin Martakies Co-op News 6 - 20 Sep 2005*

269 Unfortunately, there are many who sit on Area Committees who "just go with the herd": *"Cutting*

*back on electee training will indeed impede an ability to properly fulfil their governance function
..... I don't see a great diversity in committees and boards, - I see a depressing homogeneity.*
Chistopher Lydall: " Co-op *News* 6 - *20 Sep 2005*

270 Although there are a good number of decent, genuine and committed Co-operators, I suspect that many elected members who do not stand up to the Executive and Secretariat because of fear or have vested interests or an outmoded belief in "The Co-operative Way" (don't criticize or "rock the boat"). This may be an explanation why past Co-operators have allowed the democracy to become so weak.

271 The underlying principle of democracy is free speech. However, the CG appears to have a Control Freak Culture pervading its Executive and Secretariat **(for definition see para 446 - 449).** It is obsessed with secrecy and attempts to crush criticism. In so doing, it is undermining and destroying the Co-operative foundations based on democracy, free speech and openness. It attempts to use "confidentiality" to gag outspoken elected Co-operators. Such a victim was the late Hugh Bridge, a passionate and fiery advocate for Co-operation, who was suspended for three months for "breach of confidentiality." Alan Middleton provides further evidence:

272 *"It is however a sad day when a professional officer chooses to break with a 134 year old convention that paid officials do not engage in personal attacks on democratically elected lay directors ..... (the) Movement is already over-dominated by paid officers. .... Employees of the Movement - who will not rest until the voice of the lay member has been completely silenced. "(Alan Middleton, a lecturer and senior director in the Movement). Coop News 23 Aug - 6 Sep 2005.*

273 The Co-operative News is the main organ of the Co-operative Movement for the independent expression of views and comment. However, although it tries to maintain its editorial independence, it is under considerable pressure to avoid being too critical of the CG hierarchy. After all, it is the News's main source of its income. This pressure is even greater due to the merger with United giving control of 85% of retail co-operative business.

274 From personal experience: when I was on the SE Values and Principles Committee, I proposed that discussion groups, run along policy forum lines should be introduced, especially at Regional AGMS. The aim would be to connect elected members with ordinary members. I was very experienced in this as I had run Labour Policy Forums and the teacher training course I ran was along similar lines. This is the meeting mentioned in the **Appendix (para 402 - 404)** where the Regional Secretary (Karen Froggatt) was 11/2 hours late. The Chair, Adrienne Lowe, appeared to manipulate the agenda around my motion and slowly paced the meeting so that it was not discussed, or voted upon, by the end of the meeting. As one experienced, old timer said to me afterwards, "They didn't want it." It was clearly undemocratic. Although speculation, the Regional Secretary, who appeared to "want to control everything," would be somewhat by-passed if ordinary members' views from the forums, were documented. Ironically, Len Wardle (former CG Chair) at a recent NFPC meeting (2014) advocated such a system. When I said that I had tried to introduce it some 12 years ago he said: "That's something we CAN agree on!"

275 Although there are many issues circulating around the CG democracy, I will simply draw attention to my Co-op News, two page, and B4 article 2006: "It's Your Choice ... a Blueprint for the Future or the Final Curtain for Co-op Democracy?" **(Ref 11 p1 & 2).** The original draft is included and goes beyond the edited version. In a paper to a recent NFPC meeting, I identified a number of discussion points. I will list them, but keep the discussion to a minimum, I am sure that this issue will be raised repeatedly within most enquiries (especially Kelly and Myners).

276 *QUINQUENNIAL REVIEW PROPOSALS*   by *VIC PARKS MAY 2006*

277 *"Is the Co-op Group's Quinquennial Review an opportunity to build a comprehensive blueprint for the future or will it be a tightening of the noose on the Co-operative democracy?"*

278 *The principal aim behind this article is to strengthen the Co-operative Democracy, make it work more effectively and ensure that elected members have real influence and control.*

279 *"Ownership by the members and their democratic control is the unique and fundamental tenet of co-operative enterprise." In my view, this basic principle has been systematically undermined over the years – cost cutting such as under "Project Exchequer" has exacerbated this trend. There is considerable frustration and anger that elected members are ignored, side-lined and made "impotent." Ralph Taylor (formerly on the Sussex Area and RV&P Committees) is indicative of these symptoms:*

280 *"I joined the committee in 1999, full of enthusiasm… but after six years, I had had enough. Enough of the committee being either ignored or patronised."… "Reluctantly, I came to the conclusion that the "Democratic" processes of the Co-operative Group were largely a façade and that I was wasting my time attending the Area Committee." (Co-operative News Jan 10 – 24 2006).*

281 *FUNDAMENTAL DECISION MAKING*

282 *Even when the overwhelming majority of the South East region's elected members opposed the cuts under Project Exchequer, including the Regional Board, their protestations went unheeded. Critical decisions deeply affecting many of our members are just delivered as a fait accompli, from above, with no real consultation (e.g. closure of non-food stores, food superstores, sale of Priory Motors).*

283 *Why not consult widely amongst members and customers on proposed closures?*

284 *Could Referenda be used as part of the decision-making process? Referenda would make it "bottom up" rather than "top down." After all, when the members' assets are being disposed of or the service to them is being withdrawn, should they NOT have a say? At the very least, decision making on fundamental issues with far reaching consequences ought to be taken region wide using referenda among Area Committee members. Where possible, it ought to be extended to ordinary members, the owners of our society.*

285 *Could decisions of the Regional Board be open to challenge within six weeks of the decision being distributed in the Minutes. Perhaps there could be a system of ratification, or not, by the next Area Committee meeting.*

286 *STRENGTHENING THE DEMOCRACY*

287 *Key principles of democracy are Freedom of speech and the right to free and open discussion. Debate on all sides of an issue is paramount.*

288 *One of my deep concerns is the lack of real debate of issues and policies. Again, in my relatively short time in the Co-operative Movement, I have seen opportunities for discussion, debate, sharing experience, expertise, views, and so on gradually eroded away. For example, less*

opportunities to go to conferences, training workshops, Summer Schools, reduction of Area Committee Conferences and so on. Often, events are "Stand and Deliver" in format, based upon the "Filling empty vessels [with knowledge]" training style. The "platform" usually sits above the "audience" who are often seated in rows. Questioning is invariably formal "Stimulus – Response" style with no right of follow up questions or questioning of the reply. If one attempts this, he/she is accused of "heckling" and not of the "Co-operative Way." Several years ago, at an Area Committee Conference, I was asked by the then Regional Chair and (separately) by the Regional Secretary "You did not say anything." I replied: "What's the point?" Ralph Taylor above reinforces my view that we have very little influence or just ignored.

289 *There needs to be more REAL debate by elected members. In the first instance, there should be more opportunities for members of Area Committees to meet Region wide and with others in other parts of the country. Perhaps more "special" Area Committee meetings, in addition to the normal "business" meetings are necessary.*

290 *A computer-debating forum needs to be properly established.*

291 *The debate by members needs to be properly facilitated in a non-judgemental, open and friendly way. Offering more opportunities for face-to-face discussion is of no use if it is contrived and controlled in an autocratic way. In the past year, our Area Committee has had two opportunities to adopt a much more informal and interactive mode of discussion. Our "Blue Sky" meeting and the Half Yearly meeting afternoon session ("Burning Issues") were seen as being very successful. The key difference is that peoples' concerns are written down, recorded and agreed, even if a "minority report." Thus, there is a record to be acted upon and progress monitored.*

292 *CONFIDENTIALITY*

293 *This is particularly pertinent to the situation elected representatives are in. Given that debate is essential between co-operators for effective democracy, blanket use of "confidentiality" would stifle any debate. No one can discuss anything, being in fear of breaching confidentiality. It is suggested that written material ought to be run past the Management. Clearly, this is open to abuse as a form of "censorship." Criticism of management might be "struck out" on spurious grounds of breaking confidentiality.*

294 *Committee members need to be clear as to what can and cannot be discussed outside the committee forum. Arguably, confidentiality may be used by management to protect itself. For example, the use of "Gagging" clauses for past and present employees, to cover up unethical, bad management practices. Identifying guidelines is difficult, but a few suggestions:*

295 *Perhaps there needs to be a list of specific instances, which are absolutely confidential (e.g. store closures, disciplining of staff, etc.)[1] Issues that relate to the democratic structure and processes ought to be open and transparent. The test would be whether any breach would be of commercial advantage to a competitor.*

296 *One problem is who decides what is confidential or in the Public Domain or, indeed, placed there?*

297 *Perhaps there could be a lay, Confidentiality Advisory Panel (CAP) to help give guidance.*

---

[1] This would depend on the discussion earlier about "bottom up" decision-making.

© Vic Parks 2014

298 *Perhaps members ought to be protected by a "whistle blowing" rule (e.g. "Disclosure in the Public, Co-operative interest."), in the same way that staff are (rightly) protected.*

299 **DEMOCRATIC STRUCTURE AND ROLES**

300 *All members of the Main Board, including the representatives of the Corporate membership (i.e. other Co-operative Societies who are shareholders in the Co-operative Group), must be lay directors. As I understand it, ten of the eleven representatives of the Corporates, are Chief Officers/Executives. This could give rise to a bias in favour of the "Executive." In view of the widespread perception amongst activists that the executive or management has too much power, in real terms, this goes against the principle of the democratic control by the membership through its elected members.*

301 *Area Committee size should reflect a formula based upon the number of trading outlets, geographical size, level/type of membership activities undertaken (including contested AC elections) and turnover.*

302 *Appointment of senior staff ought to come from the ranks of co-operators. The shop floor to senior management ought to be the norm, rather than the exception. Their co-operative credentials must be clearly evident.*

303 *I am concerned to see the appointment of senior staff from outside the Co-operative Movement. An example would be the Head of Funeral Care. This is not intended to be a question of his competence, but my fear is that if this trend continues, there could be a dilution of Senior Managers who are committed to Co-operative principles and values. Added to this, senior staff in the lower tiers might find it demoralising if outsiders are always appointed over their heads. Around 1993, the then Tory Government took Further Education out of Local Authority control. A new wave of (what I described as) "Business Mentality" managers came in bringing with it an ethos of "Control Freak Management style." I saw people humiliated and destroyed, doing immense damage to morale and the educational community within FE/HE colleges. The damage inflicted then, and Control Freakery, still continues today.*

304 **ROLE OF MANAGEMENT STAFF**

305 *There is a widespread feeling that Management is firmly in control. How many examples of change (or suggestions being taken up) that can be identified as originally coming from an "ordinary" committee member? Often, when making suggestions, one will get the response: "Oh, you can't do that because...." The danger is, as in the case of Ralph, people give up – "What's the point?" "Can I make better use of my time?" The elected representatives should take strategic decisions in an informed way, with input from management.*

306 *There needs to be a clear definition of roles and boundaries – providing information but not to control outcomes.*

307 *Should the Area Committee appoint a Minuting Secretary from its own number? Perhaps he/she could have an honorarium.*

308 *This would save costs and put the committee more in control of its business. Although I realise that there is a "Standard Format" for Committee minutes I often wonder how useful they are for future reference. For example, a minute might say something was discussed but there is no record*

of WHAT was discussed. Perhaps minutes ought to be more informative for those people who are not present at the meeting.

309 *PERSONAL RELATIONSHIPS BETWEEN STAFF*

310 *In many commercial companies, intimate relationships between staff are, if not frowned upon, against the rules, particularly in the immediate workplace. Equally, when members of staff and elected members enter into intimate relationships, conflict of interests, whether real or potential, may arise.*

311 *Should a review be carried out that investigates this very sensitive issue, with a view to rule changes? (Nick Eyre, in one of his letters, states that this could be part of the Q.R.).*

312 *The age Rule needs to be scrapped. [It was, in 2008] It is discriminatory and can deprive Committees of talent and valuable experience.*

313 *The competence of members ought to be evaluated individually (e.g. some form of appraisal).*

314 *As to the costs of all this, it has to be recognised that effective democracy costs money. If the concept of Co-operation is seen as a desirable goal, the costs must be seen as an investment for the future rather than a "drain on resources." Being part of a £9B organisation, these are miniscule.*

315 *I have a dream ….. Co-operative enterprises run by collective, co-operative and collaborative people. They work in harmony towards goals guided by co-operative principles and values, whether staff or elected representatives. In this dream, people are free to disagree with the consensus, but their views are respected, without fear of reprisal. © Vic Parks 8 May 2006*

316 The above is supplemented by the following questions below:

317 It is a paradox that PLC shareholders have more rights than CG members (e.g. attend AGMs).

318 As far as possible, should there be OMOV decision making? However, it is a complex issue. How can it be achieved?

319 Would regular all member meetings, which can take and reverse decisions of Boards and committees, go some way to empower OMOV members?

320 Should ordinary members be directly involved in decision making on the closure of shops?

321 Should Boards and committees seek the permission of the all member meetings (e.g. store closures)? Perhaps referenda or postal/on-line votes would help, which happens in PLCs and building societies, charities AGMs. On-line petitions are commonplace these days. Had ALL members had had a vote (in Unite Co-op [especially] and CG, perhaps CG disaster would not have happened (Marks, would not have become CEO).

322 The CG glossy document was heavily biased in that it expounded the positives and not the negatives. Should documentations give equal space to arguments for and against an issue?

323 Would splitting regions into autonomous boards help?

324 Indirect Democracy is highly discredited, these days, and probably largely responsible for voter apathy. The delegate system (Indirect Democracy) makes it easy to control the "agenda" by powerful individuals/small groups/management. Should the delegate system be abolished? If continued, should delegates be autonomous, and decide how to vote based upon the discussion at the meeting?

325 The person who writes the Minutes of a meeting has considerable power. In the past, it is alleged that a former Area Committee Secretary was protective of management (e.g. avoided detailing criticism). After a store visit, I saw that there were serious H & S problems. It took me three meetings to get my concerns minuted and then by having to write it out in full. Sometime later, the CG was fined hundreds of thousands of pounds because a store was in breach of H & S.

326 Should the committee appoint a Minuting Secretary from its own number on a stipend? Or employ a part time one? In many organisations, intimate relationships are against the rules. Some years ago we had a situation where the Chair of the Regional Board was married to the Area Committee Secretary. Should there be strict rules regarding intimate partners (e.g. wives) when there may be a conflict of interest?

327 If the current (cynically) (UN)democratic representation decides the future governance, post Kelly, Myners, Treasury Select Committee, history is likely to repeat itself. The CG 2007 Quinquennial Review was a damp squib, after much huffing and puffing and "consultation." Out of self-interest, little will change; as the current elected members will not reform themselves **(see Para 11, Ref 16).**

328 Lord Myners in a Co-op News interview stated*: "It will then be for the Board to decide whether to accept my recommendations in total or in part and whether it wishes to put any of those recommendations to the AGM I don't have any power to put anything to the AGM..."* This is somewhat depressing and the various enquiries could be a complete waste of time. Grassroots hopes will be raised, but then dashed. However, if the Review/Enquiry was to consider legislation to create a framework for large co-operatives, there is more chance of a truly democratic structure representative of the views and aspirations of the ordinary members. There are many "Co-operative academics" that could produce a considered and objective structure, perhaps under the wings of Co-operative UK and the International Co-operative Alliance. Instead of the "usual suspects" with self-interest voting on new Governance proposals, perhaps they should be voted for on-line or through regional meetings with duplicated documentation and agendas.

329 In my "Overview, I suggest that all those in the elected bodies are responsible with regard to the collapse of the CG and, indirectly, Co-op Bank. Although a bold step, perhaps they, individually, should be replaced unless they can show evidence of standing up to the cronyism and Secretariat. Clearly, some good people would go. On an interim basis, respected, co-operative experienced members could fill the current structures (perhaps retirees).

330 When I was first elected fees were nominal amounts whereas now, they are substantial and people may be drawn in simply for the fees and "perks" (e.g. four star hotels, discounts). If elected members rely on fees, they are likely to be more easily controlled and "not rock the boat." It appears that the increase in fees may attract people who are more interested in a supplementary income plus "perks" than people who volunteer out of conviction. Some "career politicians" appear to want to put "Co-op" on their CVs, yet they are not really committed to the Co-operative ideals.

It's your choice ... a blueprint for the future? Or the final curtain for Co-op democracy?

CO-OPERATIVE GROUP activist VIC PARKS (pictured) discusses the issues which he believes should be at the heart of next year's Quinquennial Review and offers his own personal vision of the way ahead for the Group and the Movement

INSTEAD of being a measured and detailed analysis by the whole of the elected membership, the delayed Quinquennial Review is in danger of being a rushed and botched exercise.

In the wake of the postponement of the Review from 2004 until next year and the swingeing cuts imposed via Project Exchequer despite widespread opposition, there are serious concerns about the Co-operative Group's democratic structure.

Thus the review is a golden opportunity to strengthen co-operative democracy; make it work more effectively and ensure that elected members have real influence and control. In my view, the basic principle of member control being the unique and fundamental tenet of co-operative enterprise has been systematically undermined over the years. The Project

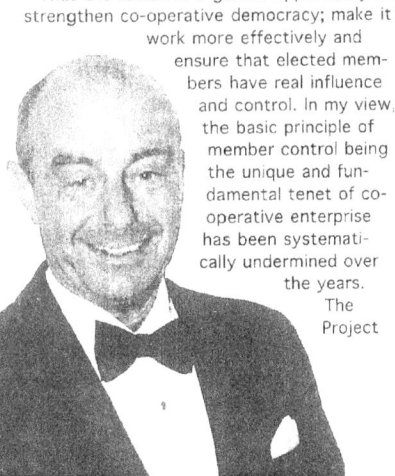

Exchequer cuts exacerbated this trend and in my experience, there is considerable frustration and anger that elected members are ignored, sidelined and made "impotent."

Ralph Taylor (formerly of the Sussex Area Committee) summed up the frustration of active members in January when he said in a letter to the News that the "democratic" processes of the Co-operative Group were "largely a façade".

Despite strong opposition and elected members' protestations, the Main Board implemented the Project Exchequer cuts.

Similar decisions (e.g. closure of non-food stores, food superstores, sale of Priory Motors), which deeply affect many of our members, were also just delivered from above as a fait accompli.

"Consultation" is often just a sham and this powerlessness is perhaps one of the reasons why there is political apathy in the wider community. Radical change is needed to address these problems. So why not consult widely among members and customers on proposed closures and why not use referendums as part of the decision-making process by the wider membership?

This would have the effect of making decision-making "bottom up" rather than "top down".

Assets

After all, when members' assets are being disposed of, or a service to them is being withdrawn, should they not have a say?

At the very least, decision making on fundamental issues with far reaching consequences ought to be taken region-wide using referendums among area committee members. Where possible, it ought to be

extended to ordinary members – the owner of our society.

And should not decisions of the regional boards be open to challenge within six weeks of decisions being distributed in the minutes?

Perhaps there could be a system of ratification, or not, by the next area committee meeting? This might help to address the frustration and powerlessness area committee members feel when decisions are handed down from above.

Principles

Key principles of democracy are freedom of speech and the right to free and open discussion. Debate on all sides of an issue is paramount.

One of my deep concerns is the lack of real debate of issues and policies. Over the years, the opportunities for discussion, sharing experience, expertise, views, and so on have been gradually eroded away.

For example, there are fewer opportunities to attend conferences, training workshops, summer schools, area committee conferences and so on.

Co-op events are often 'stand and deliver' in format, based upon the 'filling empty vessels [with knowledge]' training style. The 'platform' usually sits above the 'audience' who are often seated in rows.

Questioning is invariably formal, ie Stimulus – Response style with no right of "follow up" questions or questioning the reply. If one attempts this, he/she is accused of "heckling" and not of the "co-operative way".

So there needs to be more real debate by elected members; more opportunities for

Democracy debate must be heard

THE issue of confidentiality is especially pertinent to the situation elected representatives are in. Given that debate is essential between co-operators for effective democracy, the blanket use of 'confidentiality' could stifle any debate.

Committee members need to be clear as to what can and cannot be discussed outside the committee forum.

Identifying guidelines is difficult, but I would suggest there needs to be a list of specific instances, which are absolutely confidential (e.g. store closures, disciplining

of staff, etc.). Yet issues that relate to the democratic structure and processes ought to be open and transparent.

The test would be whether any breach would be of commercial advantage to a competitor.

I believe members should be protected by a 'whistle blowing' rule (ie: disclosure in the public, co-operative interest in the same way as staff are protected.

Given that one of our basic co-op principles is openness, it must be ensured that discussion is facilitated, not suppressed.

REF 11 P2   25 JULY 2006   B4 to A4

THE WAY AHEAD ... Vic Parks believes the review should empower members so they have a say in major decisions, such as the sell-off of Priory Motors (above)

FOUR ISSUES OF CONCERN

DEMOCRATIC STRUCTURE AND ROLES

• ALL members of the Main Board, including the representatives of the corporate membership, ought to be lay directors elected by the membership in my view. Currently, almost all the representatives of the corporates are Chief Officers/Executives. This could give rise to a bias in favour of the "Executive". In view of the widespread perception that the Executive has too much power, the present situation mitigates against the principle of democratic control by membership through its elected members.

• Area Committee size should reflect the number of trading outlets, geographical size, level/type of membership activities undertaken and financial turnover.

• Senior staff ought to be appointed from the ranks of co-operators. The shop floor to senior management ought to be the norm, rather than the exception. Their co-operative credentials must be clearly evident.

ROLE OF THE EXECUTIVE

• THERE is a widespread feeling the Executive is firmly in control. How many examples of suggestions being taken up can be identified as coming from an "ordinary" committee member? Active members often believe they are wasting their time and question the point of their involvement and commitment.

• The elected representatives should take strategic decisions in an informed way, with input from management, not be little more than "nodding donkeys".

• There needs to be a clear definition of roles and boundaries – the Executive providing information and guidance, but not strongly influencing outcomes. Members on committees are sometimes accused of sleep walking while important decisions are nodded through without proper debate or analysis. Often, this is due to shortage of time and crowded agendas. Some members do not want to "rock the boat", or do not fully appreciate the consequences of certain policies and proposals. The fundamental role of members is to hold the Executive to account.

STAFF AND MEMBERS RELATIONSHIP

• WHEN members of staff and elected members are in an intimate relationship, conflicts of interest may arise. A review is necessary to look at this issue.

THE AGE RULE

• THIS should be scrapped as it is fundamentally discriminatory and can deprive committees of talent and experience. The competence of members ought to be evaluated individually (e.g. some form of appraisal).

---

area committee members to meet region-wide and with others in other parts of the country.

Perhaps more "special, informal" area committee meetings, in addition to the normal "business," meetings are necessary.

The debate by members needs to be facilitated in a non-judgemental, open and friendly way. Offering more opportunities for face-to-face discussion is useless if it is contrived and controlled in an autocratic way.

In the past year, my area committee had two opportunities to adopt a much more informal, friendly and interactive mode of discussion using facilitators and circles of chairs.

The committee had a 'blue sky' meeting and the ordinary member's half-yearly meeting afternoon session was an open forum discussion.

Although 'open' questions were asked by the lead facilitator, the 'agenda' was set by the participants raising issues individually. Based on evaluation questionnaires, both forums were seen as being very successful.

The key difference is that peoples' concerns are written down, recorded and agreed, even if in a 'minority report'. Thus, there is a record to be acted upon and progress monitored.

Members

I would also like to see *Co-operative News* distributed more widely to members, customers and staff as a this would give everyone a better understanding of the issues that affect their society.

Reading the debate on fundamental issues and awareness of other independent co-operatives' good practice, ideas and innovation contributes to a vibrant Movement.

In addition, a computer debating forum needs to be properly established. This is particularly important for regional issues.

There is little doubt that there are concerns about the Co-operative Group, particularly in terms of its democracy, selling assets, education, training and management style.

How and in what depth the Quinquennial Review will address these issues and bring about meaningful reform is in the hands of the elected members. My fear is the 'Top Table' (through its Quinquennial Review Working Party) will filter proposals and suggestions.

It may simply tinker at the fringes (e.g. size of committees, numbers of regions, numbers of Board members and so on) without truly addressing the deep feelings of frustration and impotence many feel.

The issue is, has the Co-operative Group's servants become its masters? If so, the Quinquennial Review should fundamentally redress this imbalance.

When the documents appear, it is important that members are not presented with a "vote for it all, or reject it entirely" scenario.

Concept

Votes need to be taken proposal by proposal, preferably with options. As to the costs of my proposals, it has to be recognised that effective democracy costs money.

If the concept of co-operation is seen as a desirable goal, the costs must be seen as an investment for the future rather than a "drain on resources".

Being part of a £9 billion organisation, these are miniscule. As one of the largest co-operatives in the world, the Co-op Group is a flagship for the sector. As such, it is vital that it presents a model that all can respect and admire.

It is in the hands of the membership, at all levels, to address the perceived ills and to ensure that our organisation is deeply embedded within our co-operative principles and values, especially the democratic principle that emphasises the difference between co-operatives and PLCs.

• *Vic Parks is chair of the Co-operative Group's Surrey and Berkshire Area Committee, but writes in a personal capacity.*

What do you think?

DO you have a view on what issues should be addressed by the Co-op Group's forthcoming Quinquennial Review and how the process should work? Is Vic Parks correct in his belief that this is 'make or break' review which will shape the Group's future for generations to come – perhaps even forever?

If you would like to reply to any of the points made in these pages or air your own opinions, send your comments to: News Views, Co-operative News, Holyoake House, Hanover Street, Manchester M60 0AS or email them to: editorial@thenews.coop

APPENDIX

This Appendix is a paper presented to my Area Committee as some form of defence against the Regional Secretary's spurious allegations. I understand that three members fought for me, but the other approximate 10 members caved in to the Regional Board and Secretariat's pressure. I was forced to stand down as Chair. I believe that the Minutes produced after this meeting (written by Collette Harber, one of my accusers) were inaccurate. There were no other sanctions. There is a gap of approximately three months between the appearance of Karen Froggatt's documents and my return in April 2006 as I was dancing on a cruise ship UK to Japan, where I stayed with my son, Michael.

331 *IN DEFENCE OF INTEGRITY AND CHARACTER!*

332 *When I first started to write this defence, I did not realise that it would be so lengthy. A colleague and confident posed the question: "What am I hoping to achieve at the end of all this"? After all, this past year has been very stressful and time-consuming.*

333 *Apart from defending my integrity and my reputation (whatever that is) there is a "bigger picture." what has happened (is happening to me) is indicative of what is wrong with the Co-operative management style i.e. Control Freakery. If they can target and force me out, just for being outspoken, innovative, "radical" and standing up for Co-operative democracy, then there is little hope. They will stifle others who try to do the same. I will be on a "gibbet," a warning for others not to oppose their regime. [This goes against our Corporate Governance Code of Best practice].*

334 *I feel that Karen Froggatt's statement is a slur on my character. This has gone around the whole of the Regional Board and may well end up with the rest of the region's elected members. The minutes of the Regional Board would certainly have been circulated to everybody as part of their papers and the Minutes relating to me are certainly there for all to see (and make false judgments). I find it very sad that the RB should make a judgement on simply the presentation of one side. It shows that people have failed to see what I am trying to achieve in the years I have spent in the in the Co-operative Movement. I feel quite demoralised that I have failed to communicate what I'm about. Apart from defending myself, I feel that I am trying to get a better, more democratic Co-operative that we can use as a model for an uncertain future.*

335 *So what am I trying to achieve?*

336 *An open Co-operative Society where members feel free to voice their opinions without fear of being ostracised or threatened.*

337 *Free and open debate for proper airing of views and adequate opportunities for face-to-face discussion (e.g. more conferences, discussion workshops, training events, local forums, etc.).*

338 *A Co-operative Press where editorial content is unfettered by threat of cuts in funding, in one form or another, and to ensure that it is proper forum for national debate and analysis of ideas and issues. Proper protocols for what is, and is not, "Confidential" so that members are clear as to the Parameters without the imposition of censorship by the executive.*

339 *REAL decision making by the elected members, not just "nodding donkeys."*

340 *A membership department genuinely supporting and helping elected members. Acting as a resource (e.g. advice) rather than trying to impose what it feels is good for the Co-operative.*

341 *Change a Control Freak management ethos to one of caring, co-operation and collaboration. And more ... . Vic Parks June 2006. This page was from a summary a separate document. Below is the original document headed "In Defence of Integrity and Character."*

342 **IN DEFENCE OF INTEGRITY AND CHARACTER**

[A Detailed Response to the Regional Secretary's Allegations of misconduct].

343 *This paper is a response to a series of allegations made by Karen Froggatt (Regional Secretary) contained in a document presented to the South East Regional Board. It would appear that she is attempting to smear my character and cast serious doubt upon my integrity. I also have to say that Karen presented the paper without my knowledge and may well have misused her position as Secretary to gain an advantage, since I had no opportunity to defend myself. On the basis of this one-sided presentation of "evidence," the Regional Board passed motions, which have been widely circulated around the South East Region and have been used in correspondence by Nick Eyre to condemn me.*

344 *Below, each allegation will be a response to each point, as contained in Karen Froggatt's document. However, it is important to understand the background to this dispute and to put her allegations in context.*

345 ***BACKGROUND***

346 *Through my articles over the years and my work within the Movement, I have strenuously defended our democratic principles, ownership and control by our members (as being sacrosanct), free speech, press freedom (especially the Co-operative Press) and so on.*

347 *Ever since I was elected Chair of the Surrey and Berks Area Committee I believe that I have been victimised, bullied and undermined. However, this worsened when I had an article published in the Co-operative News 9 - 23 August 2005 opposing Project Exchequer. Initially, this was the Regional Secretary and then, by Nick Eyre.*

348 *There is a perception by others that there is a Control Freak Management style existing in the Co-operative Group, part of which is obsessed with secrecy and targeting opposition. Clearly, what I have experienced in the past year, are characteristics identified by the literature dealing with this destructive phenomenon (see Definition para 446 - 449). There are accusations that the Co-operative Group is obsessed with secrecy and stifling debate. From my sources, throughout the Movement, I understand that Nick Eyre at a National Values and Principles meeting tried to put pressure upon the Co-operative Press not to print, or at least tone down, criticism of the Group. Clearly, it is using its financial clout to frighten the Press Board, which is heavily dependent upon Group funding and purchases. I am deeply concerned that all this is crushing our democratic principles. Even in the relatively short time I have been in the Co-operative Movement (about eight years), I can see how the democratic rights, freedoms and structures have been (and still are being) eroded away.*

349 *POTENTIAL CONFLICT OF INTEREST*

350 *In the past year, I have had extensive correspondence with Nick Eyre (Company Secretary and, ultimately, the Regional Secretary's senior manager). Initially, this was to do with the situation regarding Colette Harber and her husband. In their roles as Area Committee Secretary and Regional Board Chair many had voiced concern that there could be a potential conflict of interest.*

351 *To a large extent, I was "just the messenger." I took it upon my shoulders to raise this issue, effectively, on behalf of other elected representatives. A considerable number had expressed concern about the situation. For me, the relationship was a point of principle, which was clearly expressed in my original letter to Martin Beaumont 16 May 2005, as quoted below for simplicity.*

352 *In many commercial companies, it is against the rules of conduct to have personal relationships with other members of staff or clients. In some organisations, members of staff can be dismissed.*

353 *My personal career experience is mainly in education. Until early retirement, my last eleven years was as a Senior Lecturer leading and running a teacher training course for teachers and trainers in Further, Adult and Special Needs Education, the Police, NHS, Private Sector, etc. It was my strict policy not to have relationships with my students (mostly women between 21 and 50) and other members of staff. In my view it is unprofessional and invariably undermining with detrimental consequences for staff morale and working relationships.*

354 *From my interpretation of our rules in the Co-operative Group, there appears to be no policy with regard to personal relationships. There are rules regarding membership of Area Committees regarding spouses, partners, family members, employees and so on. Nevertheless, these do not seem to extend to situations where relationships might be seen as "unprofessional, "inappropriate" or detrimental.*

355 *Nick Eyre contacted me after Martin Beaumont passed my letter onto him, who then dealt with the matter. He had made discreet enquiries of senior South East Directors who reinforced my view by stating: "There was a problem." With my permission, my letter was released to Bob Harber. He decided to defend his position, to remain as Chair. Events resolved the situation as he was later voted off as Chair (10 to 1), although not necessarily due to the potential conflict of interest issue. In my view, agreed by Nick Eyre in correspondence, this is an issue that needs airing in the Quinquennial Review.*

356 *The point of drawing attention to this is because Colette Harber was providing "evidence" in Karen Froggatt's document containing allegations against me. This will be returned to later.*

357 *ALLEGED BREACH OF CONFIDENTIALITY*

358 *As stated above, since the publication of the article opposing Project Exchequer **(Ref 1, p1),** I believe that I have been victimised, bullied, harassed and undermined in my role as Chair of the Surrey and Berks Area Committee. It was alleged that my article was a "breach of Confidentiality." I found Karen Froggatt's original letter **[Ref 6],** making the allegation, somewhat offensive. Indeed, I interpreted it as being a form of "entrapment" by demanding that I admit a breach of confidentiality. I queried what parts of the article could be seen as breaching confidentiality.*

359 *As it transpired, after further correspondence (Nick Eyre took over this issue from October 2005), the whole allegation against me rested on the name Euro Co-op appearing in the article. In my view, this was a trivial excuse to accuse me of a breach of confidentiality, as there was no damage done at all. I understand from Nick Eyre, they were not aware of the cuts coming their way. Why should this have been the case when all other organisations mentioned in the article were aware of their cuts?*

360 *When I originally wrote the article, I consulted widely at various levels of the Co-operative Movement. I was told by a very high source "everyone knows about it" and it was in the Public Domain. It had also appeared in a Co-operative Party newsletter. Project Exchequer's cuts were published in March and my article appeared 9 August 2005, some five months later. I also refrained from identifying the levels of cuts in percentage terms. I circulated the draft around my Area Committee and there were no detrimental comments, especially as to confidentiality. Furthermore, the paper received by the Area Committees, announcing Project Exchequer, did **not** contain any confidentiality or restricted marking.*

361 *I interpreted the allegation of a "breach of confidentiality as a form of "censorship," and an attempt to deter me from expressing my views in a public forum. This would have had future implications not only for me, but others wishing to begin a discussion of issues that had, perhaps, profound and fundamental effects upon the future of the Co-operative Movement. In my view, Nick Eyre's pursuit of this trivial issue was tantamount to bullying as the mentioning of the Euro Co-op caused no damage whatsoever.*

362 *However, I believe that there are wider perspectives. Nick Eyre in his letter dated 30 November suggested that there is a need to seek advice from the Regional Secretary regarding what is, or not, in the Public Domain. Clearly, where there is a commercial interest (especially to a competitor) this is valid. However, if I (or others) wish to write on a subject of potential concern or interest to members in the Co-operative Movement (that is of no commercial interest to a competitor) then seeking advice from the Regional Secretary could be seen as a form of censorship. Indeed, if management and administration were to be the final arbiter, then it would be in a position of preventing publication of articles/letters/Internet forums critical of management and its decisions. Holding the executive to account is also another fundamental democratic principle.*

363 *Given that democracy is at the heart of the Co-operative Movement, a key prerequisite is the principle of free speech and freedom of the press. Here then is the dilemma. Who decides what would be a breach of confidentiality or not. Inevitably, someone has to make a judgement. Should it be a "censor" or left to the good judgement of the author? If taken to an extreme, the mere mention of the name "Project Exchequer" in an article could be seen as a breach of confidentiality, since it is contained within "confidential papers." Yet this does not appear to be an issue with Nick Eyre or Karen Froggatt, since they considered Ron Hunter's article as NOT being a breach of confidentiality. These issues are a matter of conjecture and the Quinquennial Review would seem to be an appropriate forum for debate.*

364 *If we, as democratically elected persons, cannot effect change or become impotent, it undermines the whole Co-operative philosophy. It makes it very difficult for activists to argue for Co-operative solutions to political problems, if the concept does not work in practice.*

365 *As can be seen from the above, I have been subjected to considerable pressure, over the past year. I have had no professional help, other than friends and colleagues, in resisting the attack from the Co-operative Group senior management. Having failed to censor me regarding using the trivial excuse of "breach of confidentiality," Karen's paper attempts to smear my character by opening up another line of attack*. **b) Retaliation: the bully counterattacks. The bully quickly and seamlessly follows the denial with an aggressive counter-attack of counter-criticism or counter-allegation, often based on distortion or fabrication (Definition para 448).**

366 **FORMAL COMPLAINT REGARDING KAREN FROGGATT'S CONDUCT**

367 *In my letter 4 October 2005 to Nick Eyre, I made a formal complaint about Karen Froggatt's conduct (nearly two months before Karen's paper). This seemed an appropriate level since his deputy (Moira Lees) was Karen's line manager. I included copies of emails where Karen Froggatt had refused to carry out my reasonable requests, as Chair, just prior to the Surrey and Berks Half Yearly meeting. Since Nick Eyre fully supported Karen's actions I wrote a subsequent letter (11 November 2005) describing an incident at the Half Yearly meeting, in which, I believe, Karen Froggatt was deliberately undermining my authority, as Chair. He did not act on this formal complaint. At this point, I will provide the original extract of the complaint. I recorded the incident in the evening whilst it was fresh in my mind, so that it was an accurate record. This was reprinted in a letter 11 November to Nick Eyre:*

368 ***In paragraph three of your letter, you state that you fully support Karen Froggatt's actions, regarding my members' Half Yearly meeting. As Chair of my Area Committee, are you condoning a paid employee over-riding an instruction from the democratically elected Chair? If this is the case are you not creating a constitutional problem? There is more to this incident than simply refusing to photocopy my article [and other responses which I wanted to make available to members], and I recount this below. I ought to say, at this point, I sent an email to my committee members stating that I wanted my article copied. There was support from two and no dissent from others.***

369 ***On advice of a committee member, I had decided to ask the Half Yearly meeting whether they wanted to hear my presentation on Project Exchequer. To avoid a potential disagreement in front of staff and members, I requested a private meeting just before the start of the Half Yearly meeting. At this, Karen refused to use my disk for my presentation, stating that she was not prepared to use her (the Co-op's) equipment for my software. I had spent a day preparing for the presentation and the Power Point slides, which I had fully disclosed to her. She stated that she was prepared to allow it in the afternoon. I explained that I wanted to keep the afternoon informal, having planned an innovative session, using small groups.***

370 ***She cited the Standing Order that the agenda could not be changed. I said, as Chair in charge of the meeting, that I was going to ask permission of the meeting. She then threatened: "1 am warning you that that if you ask the meeting, I will speak" I asked her what she would say and she refused citing "freedom of speech " I asked her whether she was going to undermine me. She refused to say, commenting that I had been "emailing the world undermining her." I said that I was involving my committee, since she had kept claiming that I was not truly representing their views. It is my view that Karen was blatantly undermining me by refusing my requests.***

371 *She then accused me of "promoting myself' in wanting to give the presentation, which is clearly not true. She also accused me of perpetrating my own opinions in the presentation and not representative of my committee. I said that that Project Exchequer had serious consequences for the Co-operative democracy and that is why the members should know its implications. I said that she had not mentioned it in her original "National Overview" notes (written for speakers to read) and that Paul Sommerfield (Chair North London Area Committee) had said in an email that there was only "an opaque reference, "(indirectly through Project Chancellor).*

372 *It is clear that her stance was deliberately provocative and there was at risk of causing a public display of discord I was sure that my committee would not want that, and I decided to avoid the confrontation, which she was threatening. I was astounded that she should be prepared to threaten a public dispute over such a relatively minor issue.*

373 *Having accused me of putting forward my personal views, being not representative of my committee, Bob Harber (in his capacity as Chair of Regional Board, from the platform) made a speech putting the management view - "sharing the pain of cost cutting." This was clearly his personal view, although he claimed, at the outset, that he was asking a question of the audience. The irony is that he did what Karen accused me of-not representing the views of my committee - since his Regional Board had voted to stop Project Exchequer. Thus, his speech was opposite to the policy of the Board, even though he was sitting on the platform as its Chair. I have to say, that my Area Committee had formally adopted a motion calling for a halt to Project Exchequer and I felt that I had their authority. Constitutionally, a Chair acts on behalf of his committee. If they do not like what he/she does, then it is up to them to criticise him/her accordingly or pass a vote of no confidence.*

374 *Marilynne Burbage gave the National and Regional Report, and provided some detail of Project Exchequer. I had supplied her with copies of my notes and Power Point slides of my presentation prior to the meeting. She commented in her speech that I was going to go into more detail, later (which we had previously agreed beforehand). At one stage, a motion was adopted endorsing and supporting the actions of the Area Committee. This was passed with no votes against.*

375 The following is Karen Froggatt's version:

376 *A few days before the members' meeting I received an e-mail from Vie indicating that he wished me to photocopy and circulate copies of a Co-op News article that was the subject of communication with him regarding the view - of myself and Nick Eyre- that the article constitutes a breach of confidentiality, in that it revealed information regarding organisations affected by the Project Exchequer cuts in advance of them being informed. I refused to do so on this basis, though agreed to accede to the request that I circulate copies of an article by Ron Hunter on the same theme (on the grounds that this did not include any disclosures of confidential information). I thought that this was a reasonable compromise, though Vic did not agree and accused me of undermining him in a series of e-mails.eg, 'you have nothing to gain by refusing to reproduce it, other than personal pride. You are infringing free speech, press freedom and being un-co-operative.' He also indicated that he intended to present a Power point presentation at the members' meeting, referring to his views re Project Exchequer. I indicated to Vie that this was not on the agenda of the meeting (which had been circulated in advance, as required by Regulation).*

377 **COMMENT: My presentation was to be an objective account of what had gone on regarding Project Exchequer and other's views. This is why I wanted Karen to make copies of not only my article, but also other views in the wake of the article. As to the Regulation, it was my advice from experienced colleagues that I could amend the agenda with permission of the meeting.**

378 *He was angered by this*

379 **COMMENT: This is not true**

380 *and e-mailed me on numerous occasions prior to the members' meeting. I contacted Marilynne Burbage, who was presenting the section of the presentation which related to Project Chancellor/Exchequer. Further to our discussions she included significantly more detail than was originally envisaged, in order to try and placate him.*

381 **COMMENT: I discussed my presentation with Marilynne prior to the Half Yearly meeting and it was agreed that I would do the main presentation on Project Exchequer in the morning session and I sent her copies of my Power point slides. She was also deeply concerned about Project Exchequer and was going to modify the speech provided by Karen to include parts that I was not intending to cover. It is a falsehood to say that Marilynne did this to "... try and placate him."**

382 *On the day of the members' meeting Vie gave me a CD which contained his presentation. He said he would be presenting it at the meeting. I referred to our previous communications on the matter. He then said he wanted to talk to me in private. It is worthy of note that for the first time in my career - I had asked Owen Jell to remain close to me as we were setting up the room for the meeting. I was concerned at how Vie would behave, given that I had previously witnessed him behaving aggressively.*

383 *I suggested that Vic may wish to seek the views of the meeting as to whether they would wish to receive the detailed presentation on Project Exchequer after the lunch break, and that I would like to speak to members before they voted, in order to set the proposal in context. (My views were - and still are - that the detail of Project Exchequer is not a matter that is of interest or relevance to the vast majority of members. It is worthy of note that at the other five members' meetings in the region there was no additional presentation on this subject, and no request for it from any committee members).*

384 **COMMENT. I find Karen's statement that: "Project Exchequer is not a matter that is of interest or relevance to the vast majority of members" as being incredulous. Is this a considered view of management and does it betray a patronising attitude towards the whole notion of Co-operative democracy? There is little doubt that many members view Project Exchequer as a fundamental attack upon Co-operative democracy (e.g. Co-operative News, motions to and of the Regional Board). Thus, the membership has real and vestige interest in anything that affects the democratic structure. Indeed, at our well-attended Half Yearly meeting, the members voted, without opposition, to support the actions taken, in their opposition to Project Exchequer, by the Area Committee, Regional Board and the Region's three Directors.**

385 **As to Karen's assertion that no other Half Yearly meetings had additional presentations on Project Exchequer, it has to be remembered that Karen Froggatt writes the speeches for the speakers on the platform. Even though it was a highly controversial issue throughout the SE region, she chose not to mention it in the speeches she sent to speakers. This was criticised by Paul Sommerfield, as quoted above.**

386 *In response, Vie became angry and said he would not allow me to speak unless I told him exactly what I intended to say*

387 **COMMENT: This is not true.**

388 *Given that I was making no progress in the discussion, I ended the conversation.*

389 **COMMENT: This was the reverse; I ended the conversation, as she was adamant that she was not going to accede to my requests and her stance was designed to try and provoke me.**

390 *I had no idea what would happen during the meeting. As it was, he did not make further reference to the presentation.*

391 **COMMENT: This was because Karen had threatened to cause public confrontation.**

392 *Incidentally, in the afternoon session Vic facilitated discussion sessions involving members. I volunteered to take away the flip charts and have the content typed up and circulated, in an attempt to be helpful, and to hopefully temper his attitude towards me. However, I recently received a copy of a letter from Vie to Nick Eyre in response to a letter from Nick regarding the breach of confidentiality issue. The letter said little about the breach, though says that the 'current situation' (re the breach) was 'started off by Karen'. It focused instead on issues relating to the members' meeting. In it he accuses me of 'blatantly undermining' him and says I was 'deliberately provocative'. The most worrying (and wholly untrue) content relates to Vie indicating that I was 'threatening' a 'confrontation' and 'public dispute' at the meeting. I find Vie's allegations totally unacceptable and I am obviously concerned that he is alleging that I behaved in an entirely unprofessional manner. Not only did Vie make these allegations to Nick, the Executive member to whom I am ultimately responsible, Vie sent copies of the letter to the Chair of the Group Board and to the Chief Executive.*

393 **COMMENT: Much of my correspondence with Nick Eyre has been cc or passed on to others. I also believe that the whole issue has serious constitutional consequences.**

394 *Vie's attitude towards me (and my role) is, I believe, illustrated by him asking Nick Eyre in the same letter whether he is 'condoning a paid employee over-riding an instruction from a democratically elected Chair'.*

395 **The above tries to present an image of me as one of anger and confrontation. Throughout her allegations the word "anger" is used frequently to construct a false case based upon the cliché: "say it often enough and the reader will believe it." This is a strategy of Control Freak management that it tries to portray the perpetrator as the "victim" (see Definition). Having experienced this management style in my previous employment as Senior Lecturer, I have been extremely cautious of my dealings with Karen Froggatt and Colette Harber. I know that one does not "rise to the bait" even though their actions have been provocative on occasions.**

396 Unreasonable behaviour" is often used against people (usually staff) when they are trying to discipline, dismiss or force them to resign. As I have tried to conduct myself reasonably Karen has had to fabricate or exaggerate "evidence" in an attempt to try and build a case against me. It will be noted that most of her allegations are simply "hearsay" based on alleged conversations between two people where there are no witnesses. In such circumstances, anything can be alleged but cannot be proved one way or another. The only objective judgement of the statements rests entirely upon the apparent truthfulness or deceit of the parties making or defending the allegations.

397 Clearly, there are differing accounts of our private meeting on the morning of the Surrey and Berkshire Half Yearly meeting. I would comment that I wrote my account that evening to ensure accuracy. Recognising that Karen was being provocative prior to the meeting and was attempting to undermine my authority as Chair, I knew that it was important to record honestly and meticulously what was said.

398 Karen's account was with the knowledge of my description in a letter to Nick Eyre, which was passed onto her. I certainly did not get angry as she alleges. Knowing that Karen was creating a situation of confrontation, I sought the advice of well-respected and experienced colleagues as to the best way to proceed and deal with the situation. One piece of advice was to "keep my cool" and this I stuck to religiously. I might speculate Karen deliberately caused this confrontation to unnerve me immediately before the first Half Yearly meeting I was to chair and constituted harassment. Although Karen's behaviour created an extremely difficult and stressful situation for me, I believed that I carried off the meeting successfully as the feedback was one of the best for the Area Committees.

399 *Concern regarding the behaviour of Vic Parks. I have recently made my line manager, Moira Lees, aware of my concerns regarding the behaviour of Vie Parks, Chair of Surrey & Berkshire Area Committee, as I believe that his behaviour is increasingly inappropriate.*

400 COMMENT: Apparently, these "concerns" were only made to her line manager after Moira Lees passed on the contents of my letter dated 11 November 2005. Her subsequent allegations were part of the strategy: "attack is the best form of defence."

401 *For some time I believe that Vie's attitude towards me has been confrontational. It seemed to begin after I expressed differing views to him at meetings, primarily in respect of the format of members' meetings. On one occasion (in October 2002), when discussing this subject at a Values & Principles Committee meeting, his behaviour towards me (and subsequently towards Adrienne Lowe, the then Committee Chair), was particularly aggressive, i.e., 'finger pointing', raising his voice, throwing his papers onto the table, and ultimately walking out of the meeting.*

402 COMMENT: When does having a difference of view become "confrontational"? In 2002 I had written a number of reports on conferences I had attended: National Values and Principles conference, Co-op Group SE AGM. In these I was critical of the way these meetings were conducted. For example, they lacked proper interaction being very formal in terms of room layout (platform with rows of chairs) and question and answer (questioners were not allowed to come back on the answer). Clearly, Karen did not like

my views and deeply opposed them as is evident in her comments above. Perhaps she took this as some form of personal criticism. My motive was to make constructive criticism and proposals for change. Basically, I was advocating the use of facilitated workshops to encourage Area Committee representatives to have a proper dialogue with members. I subsequently wrote a paper headed: "Proposals for Co-operative Group, South East Region AGM."

403 I asked for this to be put on the Regional Values and Principles meeting agenda and my paper was circulated for discussion and, I hoped, for adoption as policy. I knew that Karen and Adrienne Lowe were opposed to the idea (which I had verbally "floated" in previous meetings) as admitted in Karen's statement, above. The meeting started at about 7pm. Karen failed to mention that she was approximately 1 1/2 hours late for the meeting. The Chair, Adrienne Lowe, rearranged the agenda so that it skirted around my item on the agenda. The meeting was also conducted at a slow pace, spending considerable time on items that would normally be quickly dealt with.

404 When Karen did arrive (about 8:30 pm) there was more disruption to the agenda and the meeting still continued at a slow pace. I have much experience of serving on committees and boards and I began to suspect that the intention was to drop my item off the agenda, so that it was not discussed. This is what happened, by the close of the meeting. I was frustrated by what was, in essence, filibustering. I found this deeply undemocratic and manipulative and I said as much to the Chair. As one senior member commented to me afterwards "They (Karen and Adrienne) did not want it (my proposals)." Karen's statement is also misleading by stating that I walked out of the meeting. Clearly, I stayed to the end.

405 *On another occasion - in September 2002 - he was angry towards me at an area members' meeting, after some of his fellow committee members challenged him for not presenting visual aids I'd prepared and instead giving a report that his colleagues were not happy with.*

406 COMMENT: Again, the use of the word "angry" in an attempt to try and reinforce the previous betrayal of me being "angry and aggressive," which is a fabrication. This was the first time that I had been requested to give a report back to a Half Yearly meeting. I was totally oblivious of what went on behind the scenes. I was not aware, for example, that Karen Froggatt wrote the speakers' speeches. The day before the Half Yearly meeting, I received a copy of a speech that she intended me to deliver. I did not get to look at it until late in the night as I had attended my partner's son's wedding. Karen had not consulted me in any way whatsoever about content. I felt that this was her simply "putting words into my mouth" and treating me like a puppet. The speech I gave I had prepared for myself. I arrived late at the Half Yearly as I had had problems with my vehicle and went straight to the platform. I was unaware that Karen was putting Power Point slides up on the screen that had no bearing to my speech, which probably made it look silly.

407 *I have long found him difficult to deal constructively with, though since he was appointed Chair of his area committee in October 2004 his behaviour has become increasingly confrontational examples have included:*

408 **COMMENT: Again, this is a fabrication to try and create a negative image. As stated before, I have been very careful of how I conduct myself when dealing with Karen Froggatt and Colette Harber. Having experienced Control Freak Management before, I am therefore aware that one must not provide it with "ammunition." I was very much aware of their animosity towards me and was not going to play into their hands.**

409 *Vie (in a telephone conversation with Colette in October 2004), asking 'what idiot' had incorporated a negative comment made by a members' meeting attendee in the feedback we collated. (The team member concerned was Peter Hamilton, who, as usual, had incorporated all members' comments into the feedback document produced for the area committee)*

410 **COMMENT: This is a fabrication. Karen has now sought to bring others into the dispute to try and buttress her allegations. In Colette Harber's case, she has consistently demonstrated animosity towards me and, as illustrated later, deliberately undermined me. It may be personal or perhaps due to me raising the issue of her and her husbands' roles and the Potential Conflict of interest this creates.**

411 **The language of the statements, that I am being accused of, is alien to me. Idiot," "corrupt" for example, is not words that I would normally use. In my profession, I value honest evaluation. This is clearly evident in my Half Yearly evaluation report on the afternoon session, where I give prominence to the person with negative comments. I seek to hide nothing when evaluating sessions, since dishonest evaluation is worthless. I also circulated an evaluation form requesting feedback on my performance as Chair, earlier in 2005.**

412 *his increasingly insensitive behaviour towards Colette, particularly in e-mails. Incidentally, when Vic sends e-mails to me (or other members of the team), he copies all members of his committee into the communication - regardless of the content. I find this practice very negative, in addition to which responding to his e-mail communications is taking an excessive amount of time and effort*

413 **COMMENT: I reiterate, yet again, that I have been very careful of how I deal with Colette and the way I construct my emails. I am quite happy for all sides (Karen, Colette and myself) to disclose all our emails, as I am sure that mine will not be construed as being "insensitive."**

414 **I recall Karen intervening when I made a reasonable request to be properly consulted on the agenda and for draft minutes of our AC meetings to be made available about one week after the meeting. We have had many problems in the past on accuracy of the Minutes. For example, several years ago, it took me three meetings to get what I said recorded and in the form it was stated. Other members have had similar problems. Even when I was away, Colette had to apologise in the minutes for a series of incorrect minutes (Minutes 8 March 2006).**

415 **Because of the situation with Karen, I circulated my letters regarding the Conflict of Interest and the Breach of Confidentiality issues, to my Area Committee members. Karen had accused me of working without their support. My chairing style is one of openness and transparency, a "servant to the Area Committee," although I do try to give leadership when appropriate. I have often consulted them in emails to try and get a consensus or to impart information. The emails in the run up to our Half Yearly meeting were part of that process. I was being fully open and transparent, so that they knew what was going on, as my term of office was due to end.**

416 *him referring to 'the Membership Team' in the South East being 'corrupt' in a telephone conversation with Liaquat Lal, Member Learning Manager earlier this year (though I did not become aware of it until recently)*

417 **COMMENT: I spoke to with Liaquat recently, and he was vague about the conversation he claims to have had with me. I would not use the word "corrupt" of someone unless I had strong evidence that they were being bribed or had their "hand in the till." He made it clear to me that I was not doing this with regard to Karen or the Management Team. I am very cautious about what I say and to whom. Liaquat is not a confidante of mine and I would have no reason to make such a comment to him.**

418 *confrontational behaviour towards me re matters relating to the last Surrey & Berkshire Members' Meeting (see below).*

419 **COMMENT: This was discussed in detail, above.**

420 *It is as a result of issues emanating from the latter that I decided that I need to challenge his behaviour, on the grounds that I believe that it has become intolerable. Given this and the accusations of 'corruption', I believe that Vie's behaviour to me is intimidating and constitutes harassment. I therefore wish to challenge it and am drawing it to the Regional Board's attention in the hope that action is taken to address this increasingly stressful situation. (Karen Froggatt, 8 December 2005)* [End of document].

421 **COMMENT: Karen is trying to present an image of "victim." In reality, it is the reverse as this past year has been highly stressful for me. This is a strategy described in the Definition Karen is a very strong, assertive person. She has far greater depth of knowledge of Employment Law and the Co-operative Rules and Regulations than I. There is also evidence to show that she has deliberately undermined me and tried to provoke confrontation. For example, as shown earlier, Karen put me under immense pressure in the run up to our Surrey and Berks Half Yearly meeting 2005. The persistent attack on me over the mention of a trivial alleged breach of confidentiality (i.e. EURO CO-OP), which caused no damage whatsoever, is tantamount to harassment and intimidation.**

422 **ADDITIONAL ASPECTS OF KAREN FROGGATT'S CONDUCT**

423 Early in 2005 Karen sent an email criticising me for circulating my report on the Regional Chairs meeting to our Area Committee, again, accusing me a breach of confidentiality **(Ref 2, p1 & 2)**. I

pointed out that it only went to those participating in the meeting and other AC Chairs. In addition, a report by Brian Constable on the meeting had been circulated as part of our Area Committee papers.

424 It would appear that Karen Froggatt was singling me out. Added to the later allegation of "breach of confidentiality" I found this very oppressive. This obsession with the confidentiality issue is, in my view, designed to act as a gag to deter debate and discussion. Taken to an extreme, committee and Board members will not be able to discuss anything with anyone without fear of condemnation and pursuit by Management. This is not healthy for our Co-operative democracy and may be against the Good Governance document May 2005. After all, we have a duty to question and raise issues and this ought to be in a "safe" environment. This needs to be properly addressed in the Quinquennial Review.

425 From Karen's statement, she had discussed the Half Yearly situation with Marilynne Burbage. There is also other evidence that she has gone behind my back and covertly communicated with my AC members. This appears to be an attempt to undermine my authority and might be seen as a form of Machiavellianism. One e-mail's content could be seen as bullying the member for openly supporting me on a particular policy I was trying to implement.

426 Prior to an Area Committee meeting, late November/very early December I was accused by a member of circulating a letter alleging that Karen was corrupt. At the time, I was mystified as to what he was talking about. Some weeks later, 21 December, I received Karen's email disclosing her paper containing her contentious allegations, in particular, Liaquat Lal's accusation. How then, did the member come by the information? Her paper was dated 8 December. At the time, the member refused to disclose his source to me.

427 It has also to be said that the occasional emails headed CONFIDENTIAL, I sent to my Area Committee only appeared to be leaked to Karen Froggatt, as she indicated in an email dated 7 October 2005 at 16.20 pm: *"I obviously don't need to define 'in the circumstances' given that you've elaborated on the background in the note that you've circulated."* The "background note" was a confidential email sent only to my Area committee members at 12.20 pm, yet Karen was aware of it at least within a few hours of me sending it.

428 Although Karen has singled me out, I understand that she has also been in conflict with members on other Area committees, in the past.

429 **COLETTE HARBER'S CONDUCT**.

430 As previously mentioned, Colette Harber (Regional Area Committee Secretary) has shown considerable negativity and hostility towards me over the years. Thus, I have been very cautious in the way I have tried to communicate and work with her, especially since becoming Chair. Indeed, I have been very restrained in Area Committee meetings even though she has been blatantly undermining of me and aggressive towards other A.C. members. For example, when I suggested to two Regional Managers that they might provide very short reports on the stores they were responsible for, Colette (sitting beside me) turned her back on me, positioning herself between them and myself, telling them to say "No."

431 On another occasion, she verbally attacked a member, when raising an issue in a meeting saying that our committee "was one of the most disgruntled in the Region" (or words to that effect). In the past, she also accused our committee of leaking information of a store closure in Woodley (Reading) to staff in that store; this accusation was later proven to be completely unfounded.

432 Uninvited, Colette attempts to impose her views on the meeting in a dictatorial way, which is provocative and undermining me as Chair. She also betrays her impatience and irritation with members with negative body language, sighs and comments under her breath when she disapproves of what some members are saying. I tried to get Colette to agree to attend a pre-Area Committee meeting with me, some half an hour before the AC meeting. The intention was to run through the agenda, identify important items and avoid "surprises," which had caused problems in the past. Sometimes she would turn up late for these meetings, making it very difficult. Also, she would alter the agenda without any prior consultation with me.

433 As stated earlier, there have been problems with the Minutes, particularly with regard to accurately reporting what members say. It has to be said that Colette appears to protect management by "filtering" criticisms by watering down negative comments or leaving them out altogether. For the three months 1 have been away, there have still been problems as illustrated by her apology in the minutes 8 March 2006.

434 I believe that other committees have similar conflicts with Colette. In one, she provoked such anger from a member that the meeting had to be suspended. In another case, I believe a Committee member has written to Nick Eyre - due to dissatisfaction the time it takes for issues to be responded to.

435 It is one thing for the secretarial support to offer information, advice and guidance (when requested) yet another to act as "policeman, judge and enforcer."

436 There is considerable frustration and anger that elected members are ignored, side-lined and made "impotent." Ralph Taylor (formerly on the Sussex Area and RV &P Committees) is indicative of these symptoms: *"I joined the committee in 1999, full of enthusiasm ... but after six years, I had had enough. Enough of the committee being either ignored or patronised..... Reluctantly, 1 came to the conclusion that the "Democratic" processes of the Co-operative Group were largely a facade and that I was wasting my time attending the Area Committee." (Co-operative News Jan 10 - 24 2006).* When 1 tried to implement new ideas or propose changes, obstacles were put in my way. It is very frustrating and underlines our impotency

437 This past year has been highly stressful for me. I feel very much that 1 have been harassed, bullied, victimised and undermined because I am outspoken, an innovator (often seen as a "threat to the status quo" and, implicitly, their power) and prepared to question what is going on. For the hierarchy, it appears that my article on Project Exchequer was the final straw and I had to be attacked and, if possible, ousted or silenced.

438 It can be seen that the most senior managers in the Membership Department (both locally and nationally) are lined up against me. All the allegations against me come from them. It may well be that the managers, out a sense of solidarity, may have voiced what they felt Karen wanted to hear. She was clearly going around collecting "evidence" to build a case against me. This is very

oppressive and should not happen to an ordinary elected member. Geraint Day underlines this: *"... situations (where) directors do not contribute to meetings for fear of being bullied, intimidated or embarrassed ... to occur in co-operatives is shameful"* (Co-op News 28 June 2005). I suggested some form of mediation to try and resolve matters but Karen escalated the dispute by publicly producing her document of allegations.

439   Karen's document is a personal attack upon my integrity and character. It is cleverly constructed being full of innuendo, half-truths and fabrication. I have tried to show throughout this Defence that a Control Freak management culture appears to pervade the Co- operative Group. From a personal point of view, I am sure many people would attest to my integrity and Co-operative credentials. However, if what has happened to me in the past year or two is not properly addressed, there is very little hope to stop the decline in Co-operative democracy. As is evident in many work places and organisations, Control Freak Management will pick off people who put their head and shoulders above the parapet, one by one.

440   The situation I am in is so one sided; Nick Eyre is a lawyer; Moira Lees and Karen have far greater depth of knowledge of Employment Law and the Co-operative Rules and Regulations than me. They have access to good legal advice. I am just an "ordinary member" trying to make a difference and attempting to uphold Co-operative principles. In my view, I should not have experienced what I have suffered, nor be put in the circumstances that I find myself in. There is no doubt in my mind that the management hierarchy is determined to silence me by using fear or a threat of censure. Karen even makes a threat of civil proceedings through an action for slander. How can we attract people to voluntary Public Service when they too may be subjected to the same treatment as me?

441   I deny absolutely of accusing Karen (or the "Membership Team") of being "corrupt." I would NEVER make such an accusation of someone unless there was very strong evidence. As Karen points out, there are laws of slander and libel. Being a member of the NUJ and having seen a very destructive libel action in a charity, I have a rudimentary understanding of the Law. I am very cautious about what I write and say, and to whom. Although I find Karen's management style excessively controlling and oppressive, I have had no grounds whatsoever of making an accusation of "corruption." However, in her position as secretary to the Regional Board (e.g. setting agendas writing minutes) she has the power to influence outcomes that affect an individual. In my case, the Regional Board passed motions based upon her paper put before them by her, which might be seen as a misuse of her powers.

442   It is to be noted that Karen has stated that my alleged comments were directed at the "Membership Team." The only conflict that I have has simply been with Karen and Colette. To my knowledge, I have not had any problems or ill feeling with other members of the Membership Team. Indeed, I have had good relations with other members and helped someone on a personal matter.

443   Clearly, the email traffic needs to be properly evaluated. I am sure that my requests were reasonable and show that Karen put me under immense pressure, for example, creating confrontation by refusing my reasonable requests in the run up to our Surrey and Berks Half Yearly meeting 2005, especially as this was the first meeting that I was to Chair for the members. Although I tried to remain composed throughout, I was in a very difficult and stressful situation.

444 Around 1993, the then Tory Government took Further Education out of Local Authority control. A new wave of (what I described as) "Business Mentality" managers came in bringing with it an ethos of "Control Freak Management style." I saw people humiliated and destroyed, doing immense damage to morale and the educational community within FEHE colleges. The damage inflicted then, and Control Freakery, still continues today.

445 Some of the "symptoms" of Control Freak Management is the turnover of staff, long periods of illness and absenteeism. It is not unreasonable to question why two Senior Co-operative Membership officers went on long-term sick leave (so I understand due to stress) and then left on ill health grounds. In my view, Martin Hill was an excellent Chief Officer, open, honest, democratic and a genuine person wedded to the notion of Co-operative democracy. His humility and approachability was evident to me in him stating that he was "our servant." Why did he suddenly disappear?

DEFINITION

446 I have used the concept of "Control Freak Management." A softer expression is "Micro-managing." Below are a few quotes from literature that support my view, although there are other factors that may or may not apply to the current situation:

447 *A control freak is a person who has an obsessive need to control other people or situations. Sometimes a control freak is a <u>bully</u> who wants power. Often a control freak will accuse others of having this character trait when he or she feels that their power is in decline or brought into question. Often they resort to the use of backhanded compliments, which is an often used strategy and, possibly, even a personality trait among control freaks. In psychology-related slang, control is the attempt to impose excessive predictability and direction on others or on events, often associated with lack of trust or insecurity, especially in a parent/child, partnership/relationship, manager/project, responsibility/dependency, or boss/subordinate context. In this context the term is a derogatory slang term sometimes used for extreme cases. From Wikipedia, the free encyclopaedia.*

448 *b) Retaliation: the bully counterattacks. The bully quickly and seamlessly follows the denial with an aggressive counter-attack of counter-criticism or counter-allegation, often based on distortion or fabrication c) Feigning victim hood: in the unlikely event of denial and counter-attack being insufficient, the bully feigns victim hood or feigns persecution by manipulating people through their emotions, especially guilt. The common objective of these offenders is power, control, domination and subjugation.*

449 *The serial bully has done this before, is doing it now - and will do it again. Investigation will reveal a string of predecessors who have either left unexpectedly or in suspicious circumstances, have taken early or ill- health retirement, have been unfairly dismissed, have been involved in disciplinary or legal action, or have had stress breakdowns. Serial bullies exploit the recent frenzy of downsizing and reorganisation to hinder recognition of the pattern of previous cases. The serial bully in the workplace is often found in a job which is a position of power, has a high administrative or procedural content but little or no creative requirement, and which provides opportunities for demonstrating a "caring" or "leadership" nature. http://www.bullyonline.org/workbully/serial.htm* Vic Parks June 2006

SUMMARY

450 **Statistically, Bullying, victimisation and harassment is endemic in the Co-operative Group (CG).** In 2007 research showed that roughly 20% of employees reported bullying. If representative of the 100,000 staff, it could be potentially 20,000 people. For a Co-operative, with one of its values being "caring for others," it hypocritical and needs to change. The symptoms show that the CG has a "Control Freak, Autocratic Management style," where "the servants have become the masters," especially with regard to the elected members in the democratic structure.

451 **Free speech is essential for democracy and democracy is at the heart of a Co-operative or Mutual.**

452 The Secretariat appears to have an obsession with secrecy and control. It tries to prevent elected members speaking out and to control them.

453 Theoretically, the Secretariat should offer support and guidance. However, it effectively, acts as "police officer," judge and enforcer. It is aided by powerful elected members who are "in bed with management" or just plain "quislings."

454 Elected members are vulnerable and easy to attack from a predatory management. Unlike employees, they have no trade union or legal support. They are on their own without any right of appeal. **This needs serious examination and, perhaps, legislation (see Proposals).** This has wider implications for elected members of bodies, trust/school governors, etc. and the legislation should also apply to these.

455 Threats of a "breach of confidentially" are used as a weapon to keep elected members in line and under control.

456 Part of this dossier is a case study of how a high profile elected member (and Area Committee Chair) was bullied and, ultimately, driven out.

457 It appeared to be a vendetta carried out by the (then) Regional Secretary and the Regional Board Chair. Although management led at the highest levels, it was aided and abetted by the SE Regional Board made up of elected members. This body passed motions against the Chair behind his back, in secret and without any representation which was a slur on "Natural Justice, a Duty of Care" - a right to a fair hearing. The Company Secretary and his deputy, both lawyers/legally trained, were fully aware of what was going on and complicit in the bullying, which was unethical.

458 Fear and "not rocking the boat" (a misplaced loyalty) prevents many elected members from speaking out and questioning management, **their fundamental duty.** They just keep their heads down and "go with the herd." There are parallels with the Enron, Mid-Staffordshire, Colchester, Cumbrian scandals.

459 Because of its hierarchical, top down structure the Governance is weak. Elected members on committees are reduced to being "nodding donkeys" and have very little influence on bringing about change or **real** decision making. Ordinary members have virtually no influence whatsoever. It is called: "The Democratic Deficit." On occasions, even Regional Boards were ignored.

460 The Indirect Democratic model, especially though the Delegation system, is wide open to abuse and control. It means, just a relatively few elected members/cliques/influential groups make decisions on behalf of the millions of members.

461 The CG appears to have lost sight of what "co-operation" means – "owned and controlled by its members," with Co-operative principles and values at the heart of the organisation. It needs to become more honest and open organisation that cares about its staff, elected members and its grassroots membership.

462 The fundamental Co-op principle of One Member One Vote (OMOV) is virtually disregarded when it comes to policy and decision making. Thus, there is a strong demand by grassroots members to have a real voice in the running of the CG. Suggestions are made in "Proposals" as to how this might be achieved.

463 Because all those in the elected structure are culpable in the CG disaster, there is a case that the whole of the elected representatives (with perhaps a few exceptions) should accept responsibility and stand down or be replaced.

464 Post the current Enquires (Select Committee, Kelly, Myners), little will change. This is based upon the evidence from previous reviews. Also, because of personal, vested interests, the current members are not likely to reform themselves. Any revision of the CG Rules will be drawn up by the Secretariat and it is likely to have a built in bias in its favour. As with most CG rule changes, they are simply "nodded through." In the Proposals, it is suggested that there could be a legislative framework for Co-ops and Mutuals. If the CG Rules are revised, perhaps they should be written by a body external to the CG Secretariat **(See paras 11 & 12, Ref 16).**

PROPOSALS/QUESTIONS

465 **ANTI-BULLYING STRATEGY.**

466 **To be effective, the right of free speech and criticism needs to be rigorously upheld with lay representatives properly supported, protected and free from fear of speaking out.**

467 **To safeguard Natural Justice, an independent appeal procedure is imperative.**

468 **KEY PROPOSAL: Essential legislation** for the protection of elected members throughout the voluntary Sector on Committees, Trusts, Boards whether Co-ops, Mutuals, Schools, Charities, etc.

   a) an independent regulatory body for members to complain to (e.g. FSA);
   b) an independent Appeals Tribunal (similar to those for employees);
   c) a statutory right for elected lay members to belong to a trade union (or its equivalent) to give independent support. The membership fees to be paid for by the co-operative they represent;
   d) full whistle blowing rights, similar to those afforded to staff;
   e) to stop the Secretariat using confidentiality as a means to unjustifiably gag members, a set of guidelines on confidentiality and an independent committee to adjudge what should be kept confidential is needed.
   f) Retraining/counselling of perpetrators in the bullying culture, or sanctions against them; ultimately, their removal.

469 The somewhat oppressive, CG Control Freak, bullying ethos needs to be eradicated to create a more caring, open, honest, democratic organisation run for the "greater good."

470 There needs to be greater respect for elected members.

471 The Secretariat needs to change so that it returns to its original role to give help, support and guidance to elected members; not act as "police officer, judge and enforcer" or promotes its own "agenda" or beliefs.

472 In the case of staff, Management have a duty of care. Should the CG have the same duty of care for elected members?

473 Should there be a rule with sanctions to guard against false, malicious or vexatious allegations designed to cause grief to others (opponents, disliked colleagues, rivalry, etc.)?

474 Elected members ought to be protected by a "whistle blowing" rule (e.g. "Disclosure in the Public, Co-operative interest"), in the same way that staff are (rightly) protected.

475 **CONFIDENTIALITY ISSUES**

476 Discussion and the expression of views need to be done without fear of retribution.

477 Blanket use of "confidentiality" stifles debate which is essential between co-operators for effective democracy, training and education. Committee members need to be clear as to what can and cannot be discussed outside the committee forum. Identifying guidelines is difficult, but a few suggestions:

478 There needs to be a list of specific instances, which are absolutely confidential; for example, information that may assist a competitor. Unless there is radical change, (e.g. move towards OMOV) specific areas may include: financial information relating to the CG's trading performance (that has not been placed in the public domain by the Society), development proposals, and closure/disposal proposals. The test would be that a breach is only when it would be of commercial advantage to a competitor or disciplining staff. **(See para 295).**

479 Issues that relate to the democratic structure and processes ought to be open and transparent and, in general, not subject to confidentially restrictions.

480 **Who decides what is confidential** or in the Public Domain or, indeed, placed there? Currently, it is Management/Secretariat. But that can lead to "censorship" or grounds for bullying. **(See para 296).**

481 **KEY PROPOSAL: A Confidential Advisory Panel (CAP)** made up or lay members assisted by staff could give guidance and ensure some form of impartiality. **(See para 297)**

482 To avoid Management/Secretariat hampering debate by excessive use of marking documents "confidential," they should be referred to the suggested Confidential Advisory Panel by the committee/board/elected members as to whether it genuinely needs to be confidential.

483 The CG Code of Conduct needs to be reviewed to ensure that it is not too restrictive.

484 **GOVERNANCE**

485 **Indirect Democracy** is highly discredited, these days, and probably largely responsible for voter apathy. The CG delegate system (Indirect Democracy) makes it easy to control the "agenda" by powerful individuals/small groups/management. It means that only a very small number of people (e.g. less than 100) make decisions, on behalf of millions of members, which has considerable implications for the CG. **(See para 261 -269)**

486 Should the delegate system be abolished? If continued, should delegates be autonomous, and decide how to vote based upon the discussion at the meeting?

487 It is a paradox that PLC shareholders have more rights than CG members (e.g. attend AGMs).

488 As far as possible, should there be OMOV decision making? However, it is a complex issue. How can it be achieved? **(See para 257 – 268).**

489 Would regular all member meetings, which can take and reverse decisions of Boards and committees, go some way to empower OMOV members?

490 Should Boards and committees seek the permission of the all member meetings for important changes (e.g. store closures)?

491 If ALL members had had a vote on the United Co-op [especially] and CG merger (2008), perhaps CG disaster would not have happened (Marks, would not have become CEO).

492 Could Referenda be used as part of the decision-making process? **(See para 284)**

493 Postal/on-line votes would help, which happens in PLCs and building societies, charities AGMs. On-line petitions are commonplace these days.

494 For decisions to be taken by ordinary members, the documentation needs to give equal space to arguments for and against an issue. [The CG glossy document for the CG/United merger was heavily biased in that it expounded the positives and not the negatives].

495 Should members and customers be widely consulted on proposed closures? [If they knew their local store might close, then they may increase their use and try to save it].

496 Could decisions of the Regional Board be open to challenge within six weeks of the decision being distributed in the Minutes. Perhaps there could be a system of ratification, or not, by the next Area Committee meeting. **(See para 285)**

497 Reduce elected members' fees 328.

498 Because fees are so high, it is tempting to draw in people who are more interested in the financial rewards and "perks" than those who join out of a sense of ideology – genuine co-operators. Career politicians are sometimes more interested in putting "Co-op" on their CVs, and funding, than being a committed to Co-operation. Is a genuine co-operator worth 20 times more than a "freeloader" making up a list? **(See para 330)**

`

499 **FREE SPEECH, EDUCATION, TRAINING AND POLICY DEVELOPMENT**

500 There needs to be more REAL debate by elected members. In the first instance, there should be more opportunities for members of Area Committees to meet Region wide and with others in other parts of the country. Perhaps more "special" Area Committee meetings, in addition to the normal "business" meetings are necessary. **(See para 288 – 289).**

501 The debate by members needs to be properly facilitated in a non-judgemental, open and friendly way. The use of the "policy Forum" format encourages open debate. **(See para 291)**

502 Decisions made need to be recorded **on the day** so that members walk away with a record. [Facilitators "on message" can filter unwanted decisions in final reports. Attendees are then in a position to ensure the report is true. Reports need to be circulated amongst attendees for approval].

503 All the Group's members are part of the same family. The Co-operative News is about the only real and credible forum for debate of issues common to most members. There needs to be a means to fund the Co-operative News to ensure editorial freedom – from CG vested interest and pressure.

504 Perhaps some sort of trust fund from independent investments. Copies should be available at all stores and perhaps given away free if a member's purchases exceed say £10.

505 A computer-debating forum needs to be properly established. **(See para 290).**

506 The competence and commitment of members ought to be evaluated individually (e.g. some form of appraisal). **(See para 330).**

507 **STRUCTURE**

508 Area Committee size should reflect a formula based upon the number of trading outlets, geographical size, level/type of membership activities undertaken (including contested AC elections) and turnover. **(See paras. 299 - 301).**

509 Would splitting regions into autonomous boards help?

510 **STAFFING**

511 Appointment of senior staff ought to come from the ranks of co-operators. The shop floor to senior management ought to be the norm, rather than the exception. Their co-operative credentials must be clearly evident.

512 In many organisations, intimate relationships are against the rules. Some years ago we had a situation where the Chair of the Regional Board was married to the Area Committee Secretary.

513 A review needs to be carried out regarding staff/members being in intimate relationships (e.g. husbands, wives, partners), with a view to rule changes? **(See para 309 - 311)**

514 **MINUTES**

515 The person who writes the Minutes of a meeting has considerable power. In the past, it is alleged that a former Area Committee Secretary was protective of management (e.g. avoided detailing criticism). After a store visit, I saw that there were serious H & S problems. It took me three meetings to get my concerns minuted and then by having to write it out in full. Sometime later, the CG was fined hundreds of thousands of pounds because a store was in breach of H & S. **(See para 433 - 435)**

516 Should the committee appoint a Minuting Secretary from its own number on a stipend? Or employ a part time one? **(See para 307 - 308)**

517 Minutes should be more detailed. For example, a minute might say something was discussed but there is no record of WHAT was discussed. Perhaps minutes ought to be more informative for those people who are not present at the meeting. **(See para 308).**

518 **FINALLY, AND OVERALL**

519 Should there be legislation to create a framework for Co-operatives and Mutuals, to avoid many of the problems raised in this dossier? If so, this needs to be guided by the eminent "good, nice guys/gals," who can rise above vested interests of those already in the CG structure. **(See para 328)**

520 In the Overview Section, it was suggested that all those in the elected bodies were culpably responsible with regard to the collapse of the CG and, indirectly, Co-op Bank.

521 Should they all stand down; unless they can show good reasons (e.g. they objected and voted against detrimental decisions and policies)? **(See para 329).**

522 **INTERNAL VOTING, ESPECIALLY COMMITTEES**

523 Chairs, Vice Chairs, delegates, etc. were selected by secret ballots on pieces of paper by committee members. Often, the CG committee secretary conducts the ballot, using the STV system. In the interest of transparency, the count should be overseen by the candidates.

524 **POST ENQUIRIES (Select Committee, Myners, Kelly, etc.)**

525 Documentation regarding new rules, policies, etc. should be written by authors/committees independent of the CG, to avoid the Secretariat writing in a bias to suit itself.

526 Instead of the "usual suspects," with self-interests voting on new Governance proposals, perhaps they should be voted for on-line or through regional meetings with duplicated documentation and agendas **(Para 318, 321, 322 and Para11& Ref 16 for reasons).**

527 **No matter what systems, structures, rules, guidance are put in place they can only help to ameliorate bad practice; so much depends upon the qualities, values and nature of those within an organisation. If its ethos is to be kind, caring, democratic, then the staff/elected members need to hold these values and live by them. Co-operative principles underpin the so-called "good Society." Unfortunately, many CG Co-operators espouse Co-operative principles and values, yet do not live by them.**

CURRICULM VITAE

Vic Parks

I was SE Co-op Group Area Committee member for approaching ten years and its past Chair. Also, a former member of the SE Regional Values and Principles Committee, Surrey and Berks Co-op Party Council and attended many national Co-operative Conferences, Summer Schools and training events.

I have been writing for many years since taking early retirement, at 50. My many articles have been published in a variety of publications on a variety of subjects: The Atkins Diet, Electoral Reform, Co-operative Reform, Appraisal, Protecting Whistle Blowers, Further Education, Anti-Terror Laws, amongst others. Most are around 2000 words or more. Added to this, I have had numerous letters in the press and appeared on radio and television shows, usually by invitation: The Heart of the Matter, Where is Middle England? BBC TV interview on prime time news, Esther Ransom show and others.

ABOUT THE AUTHOR.

Born 1945. As an early-retired Senior Lecturer in Teacher Training (11 years), Electrical Engineering, General/Social Studies (15 years), I have been very active in politics and voluntary Public Service for approaching 20 years (an "education" in its own right!). I am a well-known activist in the Co-operative Movement, the Labour Party, other pressure groups (Compass, Progress, CLPD, ERS, LCER) and national charity trustee. I believe that I am an innovator and often "ahead of the game." It is also said of me that I am "the person who asks the questions that others would like to ask but don't."

I am physically active and my life experience is wide and varied having travelled a good deal (Australia, Europe, SE Asia, Argentina/Antarctica}, lived in various parts of the UK, married/divorced, Single Parent Dad; a passionate hill/mountain walker, dancer (Disco, Trance, Modem Jive to Ballroom/Latin), a past member of NATFHE, NUJ. I have often acted in various courts as a Litigant in Person (LIP)/McKenzie Friend, from Magistrates Courts to the Court of Appeal (very rare for LIPs), RSPB and National Trust member. Although I might be seen as somewhat "academic," I have a very practical background as an Electrical Apprentice/Electrician, Merchant Navy, Royal Naval Reserve, teaching Electrical Engineering and still do much DIY/house renovation. My four adult children now live in Australia: James an A & E Consultant, Michael and David IT Project Managers, Amy a mother.

Most of my writing is: social, political, education, law, travel, environmental and general interest issues. I feel very strongly about democracy, Co-operation, Civil Rights and Liberties.

REFERENCES

REF 1 P1 9 - 23 AUG 2005 B4 to A4 news views 17

In the wake of the internal belt tightening at the Co-operative Group, **VIC PARKS** argues that the society's democracy is at stake.

Group's cuts are damaging fabric of our Movement

By Vic Parks

THE latest round of cost savings being implemented by the Co-operative Group are a real threat to the Group's already battered democratic structures.

A paper, "Project Exchequer," proposes considerable cuts to the democratic structure, particularly affecting elected members.

Their training, funding for attending conferences and other vital forms of "staff development" are also being cut.

In addition, organisations and structures such as Co-operatives UK, Co-operative Press, Woodcraft Folk, Co-operative Party, Mutuo, the International Co-operative Alliance, Co-op College, Womens Guilds, Regional Co-operative Councils, Euro Co-op, Labour Party and other supported groups will feel the pain as the cutbacks impact upon them.

One argument is that the Group's well documented financial problems are being used as an opportunity to further reduce the powers of elected members in favour of staff.

The irony is that elected members in the higher tiers appear to be meekly complying with the paid officials' aspirations.

My own view is if Co-op democracy does not work, we might as well give up and just cave into corporate capitalism.

So is the current cost cutting exercise a deliberate attack on the democratic structure?

The justification from "above" is that membership should take a proportionate part of the pain, because of last year's losses.

Ownership by the members and their democratic control is the unique and fundamental tenet of co-operative enterprise.

This was clearly recognised by a Co-op Group report on regional democratic structures published two years ago, which stated: "One of the key things that sets consumer co-operatives apart from other forms of commercial enterprises is the democratic structure under which they operate.

"Holding management to account in the running of the business is recognised as being at the heart of the democratic structure"

In recent years, we have seen erosion and dilution of training, conference attendance and delegations – which is an important part of co-operative education and member development, networking, etc.

At the same time, mergers have reduced the numbers of committees and members on them and reduced communications.

Under the slogan "cutting corporate costs", little is safe, as the strategy is wide-ranging.

Ironically, although the democratic/voluntary structures may be seen as being under attack, membership staff are protected, even to the extent of being subsidised by members' funds.

Paradoxically, it is proposed to reduce the number of committees and their size and frequency of meetings. This flies in the face of many area committees and regional boards having many new stores added to their portfolios.

For my committee, it was a massive increase. Added to that, we have seen a substantial increase in community dividend applications, which need our deliberations.

Under the proposals, some committees are expected to cover greater geographical areas with fewer people.

Historically, there has been always been tension between elected members' representatives and permanent staff, as an "us and them" reference in the 2003 report made clear.

In an ideal world, both parts ought to be in co-operative harmony, "in tune" and creating a resonance, which swells the message, co-operation actually works.

Unfortunately, even when there is genuine concern for the best course of action, there can be a divergence of view.

> **"Important that staff embrace co-operative ideology"**

Are we – voluntary activists and staff – here simply to "run a business" or to promote and help implement a dream for a better world, germinated around 150 years ago?

The short answer is "both". Apart from meeting the needs and aspirations of its members, co-operatives, whatever their form, need to show that they work.

This then may convince others there is a real alternative to exploitative capitalism.

In our contemporary, pragmatic world concrete examples are necessary. Wishy-washy theories carry little weight in educated, sophisticated societies.

In my view, the over arching and strategic aim ought to be keeping the aims and ambitions of long dead co-operators alive.

In a sense, each generation of new co-operators are the guardians, defending what previous co-operators fought for. Perhaps commercial staff sometimes lose sight of this.

I can quite understand a non-ideological staff member viewing a committee of idealists as a group of (elderly?) "nutters" who are not in the "real world".

This is why it is very important staff members, at all levels, genuinely embrace co-operative ideology and "walk the talk".

Arguably, we live in a complacent society. The current generation has grown up in "the good times" and appear to accept it will continue indefinitely.

Currently, there is considerable political apathy and disillusionment. However, rising fuel costs, expiring world resources, global warming etc will mean substantial economic contraction.

Thus, it is vital to maintain a healthy political organisation like the Co-op Party, which may well be badly damaged by the proposed cuts.

The direct costs of co-operative democracy are relatively small when we take into account the extensive and diverse expertise individual members bring to committees and boards.

What I admire above all else is they are dedicated co-operators who believe passionately about "the cause".

Remuneration

Since remuneration rates are relatively small, the people attracted to committees are likely to be genuine co-operators.

In my view, it is important to maintain numbers of area committee members to ensure a pool of talent, both future and current.

This needs to be extended and, instead of cutting membership budgets, they should be increased to enable more co-operative education and member contact through informal groups.

Although it could be suggested cuts might be restored in the future, it is important to bear in mind "temporary cuts" can become permanent.

And organisations such as Co-operatives UK, Co-op News, Co-op Party, Woodcraft Folk, Co-operative College need our continued support since they are part of the means to achieve our strategic aim.

There is still time for active co-operators to resist the proposed cutbacks as a final decision will not be made by the Group until the end of September.

All members need to lobby their representatives on the Values and Principles committees, and regional and main boards, seeking a rejection of these "Project Exchequer's" proposals, whilst waiting for the deferred quinquennial review when they can be properly discussed.

Time is of the essence and – from the point of view of co-operative democracy – it's later than we think.

• Vic Parks is chair of the Co-operative Group's Surrey and Berkshire Area Committee, but writes in a personal capacity.

United members should look before they leap

THE proposed merger involving the Co-operative Group and United Co-operatives is quite unusual since both societies appear to be in reasonable financial shape.

Although every United member can vote, the actual turn-out will inevitably be a small percentage of the membership as there is no postal ballot.

Ordinary Group members will not have a vote as the Main Board has decided to leave it to a small group of elected members, made up of one delegate from each area committee and regional board, at a Special General Meeting on April 28th.

Added to this, there is a "corporate vote", — usually Chief Executives of independent societies — so the principle of "one member one vote" on such a critical issue seems to have been lost.

Could it be that Group's and United's "Top Tables", fear that their aspirations might be thwarted? SGM rules clearly state that a referendum could be an option, instead of card votes or a show of hands.

There seems little doubt that Co-operative Group elected members will nod the merger through at the SGM. However, United members can cast their votes in the knowledge that little will change if the merger fails to materialise. Their society will go on as before.

The only 'losers' may be board members who would forfeit considerable hikes in fees or inflated "compensatory payments", for losing office.

Interests

Members really need to look beyond the spin and ask themselves if the amalgamation is truly in the interests of not only United and the Group, but also for the greater good of the whole Co-operative Movement?

If the merger is approved, 80 per cent of co-operative retail businesses will be in the hands of a relatively small number of Main Board directors.

Because of the power, might and track record of the Co-op Group, the Movement's "satellite" organisations such as Co-operatives UK, the Co-op Party, College and Co-operative Press are, in my view, facing an uncertain future.

After nearly ten years as a Co-operative Group elected member, I am almost in despair. Although co-operation is a fantastic concept, the Group acts like a PLC and I believe United members ought to look carefully at the Group's record before jumping on board.

In the past few years, many assets have gone, which is utterly demoralising for ordinary members

In theory, decisions are made in "consultation" with regional boards, but even if there is considerable local/regional opposition, it is ignored, as in the case of the South East and other regions.

The underlying principle of democracy is free speech. However, the Group appears to have a "control freak culture" pervading its Executive and Secretariat. It is obsessed with secrecy and regularly attempts to stifle criticism.

In my view, the democratically elected members count for little. At best we are ignored; at worst treated with contempt or abused and United members need to be aware that they could be merged into this culture.

The Group's democratic structures need radical reform to give more decision-making powers to the lower tiers and to change the ethos of the Executive and Secretariat.

United members need to carefully consider the issues before them when casting their vote. Even if they believe it benefits United, would it be in the best interests of the wider Co-operative Movement? In particular, will United members see some of their local businesses closed and the assets disposed of? Will funding be maintained in the long term for satellite co-operative organisations following a merger?

Will increases in directors' fees and compensatory payments mean that lay directors will be more easily controlled by the Executive and Secretariat'

Hopefully, I have raised issues of concern that members need to consider before casting their votes. Let them not be accused of being subservient "nodding donkeys" by later generations.

VIC PARKS (*vic.parks@ntlworld.com*
REDHILL, SURREY

David's unique knowledge of Movement is a great loss

FOLLOWING the sad loss of co-operator David Lazell, I'd like to say that he became a dear friend when we spent many a morning at my home having a coffee and a yarn about co-operative history.

His depth of knowledge, his understanding and his ability to retain and recount information was outstanding and I doubt there will ever be such a person again with that wealth.

His support to me in my role with co-operatives in the East Midlands will never be forgotten — he truly believed in and lived the co-operative ethos. Remembering again also at this sad time, Pam Walsh — another incredible person. I had the privilege of knowing them both well and thank them for enhancing my own life.

JENNY DE VILLIERS
SECRETARY
EAST MIDLANDS CO-OP COUNCIL

READERS' letters must be addressed to the editor, signed and accompanied by the full address (not necessarily for publication). *Co-operative News* reserves the right to edit letters.

Send your letters to:
Postbag, Co-operative News,
Holyoake House, Hanover Street,
Manchester M60 0AS.

You can also respond direct to an article immediately at www.thenews.coop

E-mail: editorial@thenews.coop   Fax: 0161 214 0878

www.thenews.coop

PROPOSALS FOR CO-OPERATIVE PRESS LIMITED ANNUAL GENERAL MEETING – 23RD JUNE 2007

The 2007 Co-operative Press Limited Annual General Meeting will be held on Saturday 23rd June to coincide with Congress. A time and meeting room for this meeting will be circulated with the official notice of the AGM.

In accordance with Rule 20 of Co-operative Press Rules any member may submit a proposal to the Annual General Meeting of members in writing to the secretary not less than six clear weeks before the Annual General Meeting.

The timetable is as follows:

Friday 11th May	Closing Date for Receipt of Proposals
Tuesday 22nd May	Agenda and Proposals sent out to members
Friday 8th June	Closing date for receipt of amendments

With regard to amendments to any proposals (stated in Rule 21) any member may send to the directors any amendment to any proposal appearing on the agenda or any amendment to any matter forming part of the business of the meeting, and provided such amendment be received by the Secretary at least two clear weeks before the Annual General Meeting, it shall be circulated to members as soon as is practicable as an additional business paper for consideration at the meeting.

By submitting a proposal, members are committing themselves to attend the Annual Meeting if their proposal is accepted onto the Agenda.

Ray Henderson
Secretary
Co-operative Press Limited
Holyoake House
Hanover Street
Manchester M60 0AS

REF 2 P1

To: vic.parks@~~~~~~~~
Cc: colette.harber@co-op ~~~~~~ ; bobharber@~~~~~~~~
Sent: Wednesday, April 06, 2005 12:37 PM

Subject: Chairs' meeting

Vic

As you'll see from the Minutes of last week's Regional Board meeting. I was asked to communicate with you re concerns which resulted from you circulating your notes of the above.

In essence, these related to the following:

- the inclusion of sensitive information in your notes, ie, re Alan Harvey referring to him having experienced difficulties in handling a disruptive member at one of his committee meetings. When Alan shared this with others, he wouldn't have expected this to be expanded upon outside the gathering. You'll note that I referred to the matter in the notes of the meeting, though not in detail
- the assumption that (given the comments in your e-mail) you had not appreciated that such meetings have no constitutional power and are essentially forums for the exchange of ideas and good practice
- the view that in future the Chair should indicate that the Chatham House Rule should apply, enabling people to speak freely and openly and avoiding any confusion as to the nature of the meeting.
  - o It is customary for me to produce and circulate notes of these meetings. As with any such notes they're a report on discussion topics and outcomes; they're not verbatim and I avoid going into detail about any sensitive issues or similar. I would hope that these would suffice as a full and accurate account of proceedings, which was a view also expressed at the Regional Board meeting.
  - o • Incidentally, thought I'm sure you're familiar with the Chatham House Rule, I attach a useful paper.
  - o Regards
  - o
  - o • Karen

        - Karen Froggatt
        - Regional Secretary
        - the Co-operative Group - South East Region, 40 Orchard Street, Dartford, Kent DA1 2DG. Tel 01322 321252 Fax 01322 321259

REF 2 P2

******** Dear Karen

I have very little time to respond fully. However, I believe that this criticism is unwarranted. As far as confidentiality goes, my email was only circulated amongst those members of ACs who were at the Chairs Meeting. I was representing my committee and my report was for their eyes. They too, are bound by confidentiality and I highlighted this to them in my paper. Written reports, as far as I know, is the encouraged policy. Indeed, we received a report on the same Chairs Meeting from Brian Constable dated 5 February 2005, for Kent East with our Area Committee papers)Agenda item 7c ii). It would appear that he was also unaware of the "Chatham Rules."

As to the Kent East incident, I also couched my reference to this in a guarded way

The fact that you produced Minutes might imply that the meeting had some constitutional power. These were circulated around the Area Committees. I have no doubt that if it suited an individual, I am sure that they would refer to them for any future argument to support their case.

I have to say, I thought that we were a "team" of co-operators trying to improve things. One of the ways that this can be done is to share ideas This is one of the reasons why I write for the Co-operative News. It has often been said that I'm an "innovator" and "the person who will ask the questions that others would like to ask but don't." In such a role, I am very much aware that innovators are often held with suspicion and resentment from conservative hierarchies. History is littered with them - Galileo, Marks, Darwin, Martin Luther King ..... It is a cross I have to bear, in my small way, trying to contribute to a better society. There are serious problems in the SE and nationally. Burying them in sand, brushing them under the carpet is a recipe for disaster. Why is the attendance poor a AC Conferences? Is it because people feel that they are! a waste of time? This is a view that I expressed to you, and Bob Harber, several meetings ago, when you asked "You didn't say anything?" I said, "What's the Point?"

I raised in my email and report that there should be a "breakdown of costs of democracy:' If "Corporate Cost cutting" is to continue, I believe that we ought to have a detailed breakdown of the Regional Budget, and I formally request this.

"Blue Sky thinking" could be an important activity for the development of Area committees.

I have to say, similar to Martin Hill's comment, I am a servant of my committee, the democratically elected representatives of the membership. It is seems odd to say that I cannot report back to the members of the committee I represent!

Regards

Vic

PS I shall be away for a week or two. I can be reached by email onmyccaccount abovevic...parks@

-- Original Message ----

From: Karen.Froggatt@co-op

****
****
********* victor parks

From: Karen.Froggatt
To: <vic.parks@
Cc: <colette.harber@co-op.
Sent: 06 April 2005 19 13
Subject: Re: Chairs' meeting

Vic

Please do not interpret the comments as an attempt to stifle discussion. If that was the case such meetings wouldn't be held; I'm not aware that any other regions hold them.

I don't understand why you received a report from Brian Constable and will investigate that, it sounds as if it was circulated in error, as it is not the norm to circulate one committee's papers to others (we already have some elected members expressing concern re the volume of paper we circulate re their own business) Elected members are encouraged to report back to their committee; that has not been taken issue with.

I also accept that you circulated your notes to attendees, but you also suggested that they in turn circulated them (hence the matter being raised)

I take on board your point that the Chairs' Meeting appears to have more 'clout' than it actually has. I'll record the outcomes in the form of notes in future

With regard to AC Conferences, we act on feedback, and I circulate all comments (as is the case with any evaluation we undertake) to members of the Regional Board.

'Blue sky thinking' is encouraged. Area Committees can undertake such discussions formally (if they have time at meetings) or informally. It's their call. We obviously also have open sessions at AC Conferences, AGMs. Half-Yearly meetings etc etc.

With regard to the 'costs of democracy'. regional budgets have been provided to the Regional Board. With regard to your own committee, Colette can provide you with details of democratic and activity costs if required (the latter is being reported on at tonight's meeting). With regard to the national costs, these will be considered by the Group Board's Values & Principles Sub-Committee in late April, further to which their recommendations will be considered by the Group Board in May.

Regards
Karen

Karen Froggatt
Regional Secretary

the Co-operative Group - South East Region, 40 Orchard Street, Dariford, Kent DA 1 2DG. Tel 01322321252 Fax 01322321259

REF 3 P1

**REPORT ON SE CHAIRS' MEETING 4 FEBRUARY 2005
BY VIC PARKS (S & B AREA COMMITTEE CHAIR).**

The numbering of paragraphs is the same as the agenda numbering.

I had to travel from Oxford to Croydon, as my son had had a second operation early in the morning. I hit heavy traffic and hold-ups, which made me about 15 minutes late. I therefore missed the first three agenda items.

The "Notes of the 2004 meeting" (supplied to me prior to the meeting) were interesting in that they raise some issues, which we have recently considered. I thought that it would be useful to make a copy available for other AC members. As with most of our papers, they are confidential. I have indicated *in italics* extracts that might be worthy of discussion by us. (See "Blue Sky thinking," paragraph 8).

4b. The trading situation of the Food Retail is not good and the CIS has considerable problems. Some of these have been addressed in the Co-op News.

4c. Cuts raised its ugly head and I am particularly concerned about possible threats to the elected member structure (e.g. reduction in committee size). I requested a breakdown of the costs of democracy so that we are in a better position to assess where cuts need to be made, if necessary.

4d. It appears that a Kent committee had a rather "heated" exchange at one of their meetings. I cannot recall one on our committee, even though we sometime have different views. The suggestion was the Chair should adjourn to let things cool down.

6. Monitoring loss-making units is high on our AC agenda, and is problematic. Even though I have reservations about "league tables" (especially in Education), I floated the idea as to whether they could help us monitor loss-making units. I do not think that some other members really understood what I was saying, but I will try again. Basically, the individual convenience/ Market town stores, etc would be placed in rank order with the best performer at the top and the worst at the bottom. Crudely, the table could be based on positive or negative contribution, although a more complicated formula involving Leakage and Wastage could be used. Indeed, these could be in separate tables.

7. I raised the matter of circulating our details between all S.E. A.C. members. As you will recall, KF sent out a questionnaire. It seems that the replies has produced a level of confusion and concern under the Data Protection Act. For example, that some committee members do not want any details disclosed to anyone. Others are reluctant to have their details accessible so that ordinary members could contact them. This seems rather odd, in the sense that we are supposed to be their democratic representatives. Some agreed with me.
KF is still collating the data.

It was agreed that there should be greater communication between committees. I suggested that Chairs might visit other ACs, as observers. This was thought to be a good idea from Bob Harber (Chair).

I also suggested that those who do not already have access to the Internet/e-mail ought to be provided with basic equipment and training. Mark Harling said that here was a rumour that there is a fridge/freezer full of redundant laptops. I suggested that the Phone Co-op provides a

REF 3 P2

relatively cheap, basic connection, although Broadband needs not be necessary, if accessing the Co-op email system.

8. North London stated that Half Yearly meetings were boring with little interaction. Perhaps there is still hope for a revival of my idea for PROPER interactive workshops (properly facilitated), which I wrote a paper on some time ago!

Karen Froggatt said that Half Yearly meetings should be amalgamated with the Area Committee meeting. If you recall, we had a short AC meeting at our ½ yearly, but simply for annual elections (Chair, delegates, etc.).

Len Wardle said that Sussex AC was intending to have an informal meeting for "Blue Sky Thinking." This would be unofficial with the agenda set by the committee and notes taken by an AC member to save the Committee Secretary having to attend. The intention would be, for example, to discuss issues that we often do not usually get time to examine in our formal meetings. **In my view, it is worth considering.**

9. It was also suggested/agreed that, where there are vacancies, they should be filled by co-option, with the co-opted person standing at the next annual election.

10d It was also agreed that delegates ought to report on the conferences, etc they attend. I half-heartedly suggested that they should not get their expenses unless they do, as an incentive. In last year's notes (2004) 2f suggests that a template would be circulated, but when I raised this, there did not seem to be much support for this previously agreed idea.

I discovered that there had been some "training" for volunteers, only the day before. I had sent in my details by FAX and hard copy but it appears that they were "lost." Thus, I did not receive notice of the sessions.

Vic Parks

28 February 2005

Group targets staff bullies

THE Group has reiterated its zero tolerance policy in relation to the bullying and harassment of employees.

Director Graham Bennett told the AGM that reported instances of bullying had dropped by three percentage points to 18 per cent of those employees who had contributed to the society's confidential Talkback initiative.

Mr Bennett said that a Respect Works programme introduced two years ago in response to findings of the 2004 Talkback survey had improved the overall situation, but he warned: "There is still much to do."

In answer to a question from South East Region, he said a Group-wide policy had been established which included a series of training interventions.

"The programme aims to encourage an environment where issues are resolved amicably and informally before embarking on a formal complaints process," said Mr Bennett. "In this way, dealing with issues should become part of the natural way of treating each other with respect.

"Support can be provided from HR or the line manager. In addition, Respect Champions have

been established as a team of people from across the Group who have received specific briefing.

"They are there to provide informal advice and the Employee Assistance Programme provides additional support through counselling and advice by telephone or face-to-face consultation."

Behaviour

Mr Bennett explained that around 80 per cent of employees have undergone a basic training programme, which focuses on appropriate and inappropriate behaviour, while a two-hour intensive engagement programme had been developed in response to the 2005 Talkback findings.

In addition, a series of half-day events had been held to help senior management across the Group's businesses create a positive climate aimed at eliminating bullying and harassment.

Concluded Mr Bennett: "Progress is being made and the Executive remains committed to a zero tolerance policy. Talkback remains the best indicator of whether we have genuine issues around bullying and we are determined to provide support in addressing this issue."

Anima on ag

DELEGATES were assured at the AGM that all fresh meat and poultry sold under the Co-operative label is produced according to strict animal welfare guidelines.

Replying to a question from the Scottish Regional Board, Deputy Chair Terry Morton expla independently audited a national Farm Assuranc Assured Food Standard

In addition, said Mr M assessments follow up o welfare to address issue ance schemes.

He added: "We have a meat and poultry. This c pork, turkey, duck and – — all chicken.

"Where we have to sc ensure product availabil Zealand lamb — this me comply with the same s and farm assurance as and, again, is independe

Membership revival strategy needed

A MOTION calling on the Group Board to review its broad membership strategy and ensure adequate levels of funding to cope with burgeoning membership numbers was carried unanimously.

Proposer Chris Hall of Wales and Borders Region congratulated the main board on its achievement of aligning membership with brand and said that participative membership is the foundation of a truly effective co-operative.

Replying on behalf of the board, Deputy Chair Steve Watts said that, in addition to more traditional approaches, new ways of engaging with a mass membership have been tried, including the

appointment of the Group's first online Co-operative Affairs Officer.

Mr Watts added that, in relation to funding, the Wales and Borders motion would be considered by Group's the Values and Principles Committee at its meeting in July.

● The annual meeting, which was attended by 139 delegates representing 25 societies and eight Co-operative Group regions, approved the following distributions among members and employees: Corporate distribution — £15.1m; individual distribution — £14.9m; community distributions — £2m; and employee distributions of £6.3m.

Call to Fairtrac

THE Group is to explore the possibility of asking the Government to make all Fairtrade products VAT free in an attempt to boost developing countries — but admits the idea is unlikely to succeed.

The suggestion that the Group should try to influence Government policy was made by Scottish Regional Board representative Struan Ferguson, who said that making Fairtrade and Traidcraf products zero rated would significantly

John Lewis is different to a member co-op

A STAFF incentive scheme on the lines of the one operated by the John Lewis Partnership, owners of Waitrose, has been ruled out by the Group, at least for the time being.

North East Regional Board member Keith Anthony asked if the Group/United merger would be the right time to introduce a bonus scheme to motivate amd reward store staff members.

as consumers to become members in order that they may share in our profits," said Mr Watts.

"As our pre-tax profits have increased to £318 million, we plan to make payments to members totalling £42.3m, compared to £27.6m paid from 2005's profits.

"I am delighted to announce that this sum includes a payment of £150 to colleagues who are

REF 5

Victor parks

From   Karen. froggatt@co-op.~~●●●●●~~>
To: <vic. parks@~~●●●●●●●~~>
Sent: 11 August 2005 13:28

Subject: Co-op News article

Vic

Having read your article in the latest edition of Co-op News, I thought it appropriate to drop you a line in respect of it.

It is obviously your prerogative to write to Co-op News and I note that the latest article indicates that it is written in a personal capacity. However, it includes information which was provided to you in your capacity as an elected representative. Please be cautious in this respect, as you could be considered to be breaching confidentiality.

Further to this, there's an issue in respect of sensitivity and timing. How do you know that the organisations affected by the cost savings have yet been notified? For example, at a regional level I'm expecting representatives of our Guild branches to make contact with me, expressing concern at what's in the article. (They haven't been advised of any cuts in funding as we hope to achieve savings in this region by 'natural wastage', given that at least one branch usually closes each year).

There's also an issue regarding accuracy. You refer to the Woodcraft Folk being affected. This isn't the case in 2005 & 6 (and will be reviewed in 2007) given concerns regarding the impact on the Folk's finances of the reduction in funding from other sources.

Regards

Karen

Karen Froggatt
Regional Secretary

the Co-operative Group - South East Region, 40 Orchard Street, Dartford, Kent DA 1 2DG. Tel 01322 321252 Fax 01322321259

This message may contain confidential information and is intended only for the individual or enti mail. Please notify the sender immediately bye-mail if you have received this e-mail by mistake free as information could be intercepted, corrupted, lost, destroyed, arrive late or incomplete, or c The sender therefore does not accept liability for any errors or omissions in message or its conten operative Group reserves the right to intercept e-mail received and sent. By sending e-mails to ar mail correspondence for assessment of compliance with the Co-operative Group published rules.
* *

the Co-operative Group

40 Orchard Street,
Dartford, Kent DA1 2DG

South East Region

Tel. 01322 321252
Fax: 01322 321259
karen.froggatt@co-op
Website: www.co-op.co.uk

2 September 2005

Mr V A Parks
1 Kiln Walk
Redhill
Surrey RH1 5SW

Dear Vic

Co-op News article

On 11 August I sent you an e-mail regarding the above, which I assume you received. The e-mail related primarily to my concern that your article contained information of a confidential nature.

I have had discussions with Nick Eyre, Group Secretary, in respect of the article. Nick confirmed that as the information you referred to was provided to you in your capacity as an elected representative of the Co-operative Group, inclusion of it in the article constitutes a breach of confidentiality, which therefore contravenes the Code of Conduct relating to elected members.

I sincerely hope that you recognise this and ask you to confirm the following to me in writing as soon as possible:

- that you acknowledge that the article contained confidential information

- that you will refrain from disclosing confidential information in future.

I look forward to hearing from you.

Yours sincerely

Karen Froggatt
Regional Secretary

cc Nick Eyre, Group Secretary

INVESTOR IN PEOPLE

Co-operative Group (CWS) Limited, New Century House, Manchester M60 4ES. Registered Number 525R
Printed on 100% recycled paper from post consumer waste using a totally chlorine-free process

REF 7

Vic Parks

From: <Karen.Froggatt@co-op███████
To: <vic. parks@█████████████
Cc: <dudley.jo@█████████
Sent: 21 December 2005 12:08
Attach: Vic Parks - RB paper. doe

Subject: Issue considered by the
Regional Board

Vic

I thought it appropriate to advise you that at the recent Regional Board meeting consideration was given to a paper produced by me, in which I outlined my concerns regarding aspects of your behaviour towards me. I attach a copy of the paper for information.

The Regional Board expressed concern regarding the content and agreed to refer the matter to Surrey & Berkshire Area Committee, asking the Committee to give it serious consideration and report back to the Regional Board regarding the outcome of those discussions. The paper, plus a covering note, will be circulated to members of your committee with the agenda for the next meeting.

It is obviously appropriate that the Area Committee's consideration of the matter is Chaired by Dudley, the Committee's Vice-Chair, therefore I am copying this e-mail to Dudley.

I believe that you will be absent from area committee meetings for a period, though am not sure whether this includes the meeting to be held on 4 January. If so, the Committee may wish to defer consideration of the matter until you are able to be present.

Regards

Karen

Karen Froggatt
Regional Secretary

the Co-operative Group - South East Region, 40 Orchard Street, Dartford, Kent OA1 20G. Tel 01322 321252 Fax 01322321259

2. ISSUES RELATING TO THE AREA COMMITTEE CHAIR

(a) **Outcome**

At this juncture, the Area Committee Secretary left the meeting. Mike Hedgethorne and Vic Parks also left the meeting until re-called into the meeting.

The Area Committee Secretary re-joined the meeting. The Acting Chair provided the following statement:

The Committee unanimously agreed that Vic Parks had breached the Code of Conduct by:

(i) *failing to fulfil his duties and responsibilities as Chair of the Surrey and Berkshire Area Committee*

(ii) *failing to carry out the decisions taken by the committee.*

The Committee:

- *requested that he stand down as Chair*

- *reminded him of its previous decision, which required him to write a suitable letter to the Regional Secretary, in the spirit of co-operation moving towards closure in respect of the complaint made.*

In accepting the decisions of the committee, Vic Parks:

- *stood down as Chair*
- *agreed to write a suitable letter to the Regional Secretary*
- *noted that the letter should be received, by her, before the next Regional Board meeting on Thursday 29 June 2006.*

REF 9 P1

the Co-operative Group

P.O. Box 53, New Century House,
Manchester M60 4ES

Direct Line: 0161 827 5185
Direct Fax: 0161 832 6388

Tel 0161 834 1212 Fax 0161 832
website www.co-op.

NAE/pdh

9th May 2006

Mr V Parks

Redhill
Surrey
RH1

Dear Vic

Thank you for your letter of 27th April 2006.

As you are aware, the Regional Board in December 2005 resolved as follows:

The Regional Board considered a paper produced by the Regional Secretary, outlining her concerns regarding the behaviour of Vic Parks, Chair of the Surrey & Berkshire Area Committee.

The matter was discussed in detail. The content of the Regional Secretary's paper was noted with deep concern. A motion expressing support for, and full confidence in, the Regional Secretary and the Membership Team was proposed and was adopted unanimously.

It was agreed that Surrey & Berkshire Area Committee would be asked to give detailed consideration to the matters raised by the Regional Secretary at the earliest opportunity, and report back to the Regional Board on their views and on any action to be taken in respect of the issues raised.

Subsequently, Dudley Smithers, the Area Committee Vice Chair, contacted Moira Lees and, as part of that discussion, an informal facilitated meeting between yourself and Karen was proposed by Dudley on the basis that it appeared appropriate to "build bridges" in a constructive manner. Moira was prepared to accept this as a way forward. The purpose of the facilitated meeting was to explore ways of, as I say, building a positive relationship going forward between yourself and the Regional Membership Team, including considering respective roles and responsibilities in an

INVESTOR IN PEOPLE

Co-operative Group (CWS) Limited, New Century House, Manchester M60 4ES. Registered Number 525R
Printed on 100% recycled paper from post consumer waste using a totally chlorine-free process.

REF 9 P2   1

In view of the circumstances, an impending **Regional Board meeting, I am sending this letter by fax and would appreciate a reply as soon as possible.**

                                                Tel:
REDHILL   Mob:
Surrey
RH1

                                             12 May 2006

Nick Eyre
The Co-operative Group
New Century House
MANCHESTER

Dear Nick

Thank you for your letter dated 9 May 2006.

With regard to the quotations from Regional Board Minutes, these motions were passed without any representation on my part either written or oral. Clearly, as Karen Froggatt is the Secretary to the Regional Board it would seem inappropriate, prejudicial and unjust for her to sit in on those meetings when she is making allegations against me. It could be argued that it was a misuse of her position to gain an advantage. In addition, the Chair of the Regional Board (Adrienne Lowe) is a party to the allegations made in Karen Froggatt's document. This is the part referring to the Regional Principles and Values meeting, which she chaired at the time. As you are fully aware, Karen's document came after my formal complaint to YOU about HER behaviour towards me. Indeed, I feel very strongly that it I who is being bullied and undermined in my role as Chair.

Karen has sought to involve members of the management in trying to build a case against me. This is why I feel that arbitration from an outside, independent body or individual is necessary. As I understand it, there are no laid down rules or Regulations for the current circumstances we are in. **IS THIS THE CASE?**

I have to say, that the impasse with regard to the mediator is also on you side and not solely upon mine, as implied in the wording of your letter. Implicitly, you have refused my offer of approaching Co-operatives UK or Alan Middleton who is widely respected throughout the Co-operative Movement as being impartial. I do not feel, in the circumstances of ad hoc arrangements, that I will get a fair hearing, especially if the matter goes back before the Regional Board. By making its statement, which you quote, it could be argued that it has prejudiced itself in any future hearings of the allegations on both sides.

I would also comment on Liaquat Lal that in my conversation with him he **WAS** vague about the date and what was said. As he said, "It was a long time ago." It was certainly more than "some months" and was well over a year perhaps two. I have to say that if this is placed in the Public Domain, the fact that an educational manager is prepared to "Give evidence against a "Student" has considerable consequences for trust between tutors and students. As a Teacher Trainer, trust is an important prerequisite between teachers and students. Non-prejudicial debate and discussion in training sessions is very important. As I recall when I attended a Summer School at Wyboston some three years ago, Liaquat was drinking and socialising with the students. If "evidence is being taken down and may be used against a student" this has considerable implications for future educational events.

REF 9 P3   2

I note that you have not answered my questions in my last letter and I re-list them below. I would appreciate a prompt reply as I am in the process of drawing up a statement rebutting Karen's allegations.

1. In the circumstances (especially in view of the threat of litigation), am I entitled to legal representation?
2. What support is available for elected representatives? Clearly, I am disadvantaged since you are a lawyer and Moira Lees and Karen Froggatt are highly conversant with "The Rules" and their interpretation, since that is part of their job.
3. As an elected representative, do I have indemnity (e.g. insurance) to cover a potential claim against me?
4. Clearly state what damage the article did.
5. How is Colette involved in the dispute (reference top of your page 2, 3 March letter)?
6. Were you and/or Moira Lees fully aware of the steps Karen was taking at each stage of this dispute?

I note that there is a proposed Rule change at the SGM, with regard to indemnifying directors and officers Rule 181. Should not this apply to members on elected bodies, in the interest of equality?

I suggest that in the circumstances – the high level of allegations on both sides- against Regional Secretary and an Area committee Chair, and the prejudicial decisions of the Regional Board and Karen's role on it, that an independent body outside the Co-operative Group hears the dispute. It is clear from your letter that we are moving towards a formal hearing.

Yours sincerely

Vic Parks

the Co-operative Group   P.O. Box 53, New Century House,
                          Manchester M60 4ES

Direct Line: 0161 827 5185
Direct Fax: 0161 832 6388

NAE/pdh   Tel 0161 834 1212 Fax 0161 832 6388
                                                     website www.co-op.co.uk

12th May 2006

Mr V Parks
1 Kiln Walk
Redhill
Surrey
RH1 5SW

Dear Vic

Thank you for your fax of today's date which you have already followed up with a phone call asking for an urgent response.

I fear you are rather missing the point. I think wisely, in your absence, your Area Committee have sought to move this matter on. We are not in an adversarial process but in light of the clear view taken by the Regional Board, your Area Committee have sought, I think in the best traditions of Co-operation, to conciliate and build bridges. To her credit, Karen, on behalf of herself and her team, has been prepared to be receptive to such an approach. If you really insist on raking over your actions in detail and force the issues, I do not think, from my attendance at the South East Board meeting, that you enjoy support in your Regional Board and you are aware of the concerns that have been raised by staff concerning your behaviour.

We can, if you want, revisit all these matters but I am unsure whether this would necessarily be in your best interests. I will pass on your letter but, on the basis that if, as appears your present wish, you adopt an adversarial position, I envisage I will need to be involved in the process. I, therefore, feel my continued involvement in this correspondence inappropriate. I have sought to develop a non-confrontational way forward but I sense I have had little success with you to date in this. I have, therefore, asked Moira Lees to respond to your letter. If, however, you feel a facilitated meeting, as previously proposed, with Karen would help I am happy to resurrect this proposal.

Yours sincerely

Nick Eyre
Group Secretary

INVESTOR IN PEOPLE

Co-operative Group (CWS) Limited, New Century House, Manchester M60 4ES. Registered Number 525R.
Printed on 100% recycled paper from post consumer waste using a totally chlorine-free process.

© Vic Parks 2014

REF 10 P1

Strictly private & confidential

3 July 2006

Mr V A Parks
1 Kiln Walk
Redhill
Surrey RH1 5SW

Dear Vic

Concerns regarding your conduct

At the Regional Board meeting held on Thursday 29 June discussion took place regarding the above, with reference to the outcome of the Surrey & Berkshire Area Committee meeting held on Wednesday 7 June.

The Regional Board noted that the Area Committee had asked you to send a 'suitable letter' to Karen Froggatt and we considered the content of your letter to her dated 18 June. Although the Regional Board did not feel that the either the tone or content of the letter was written in the 'spirit of co-operation', we agreed to note it at this juncture, and will interpret your comments as an apology.

As you are aware, the Regional Board has been extremely concerned regarding aspects of your conduct and asked Surrey & Berkshire Area Committee to give full consideration to the matter and to report back to the Regional Board regarding its intended action.

Having given full consideration to the matter, the Regional Board has agreed that in the circumstances, not least the impact that this issue is having on the effectiveness of your committee and the fact that you are no longer Chair of the Committee, it is appropriate to 'draw a line' under it at this time. However, I must emphasise that we will not tolerate a repetition of the conduct which led to it being referred to the Regional Board, and will resume our deliberations without delay if this is the case.

I will be communicating the outcome of the Regional Board's deliberations to Dudley Smithers, in order that he can report it at the next meeting of the Area Committee.

The Regional Board looks forward to a constructive and co-operative relationship with you going forward.

Yours sincerely

Adrienne Lowe
Regional Chair

REF 10 P2

1 Kiln Walk
REDHILL
Surrey
RH1 5SW

Adrienne Lowe (Regional Chair)   16 September 2006
████████████
LANCING
West Sussex
BN15 ████

Dear Adrienne

I am responding to you letter dated 3 July. Perhaps you would clearly define what is meant by: "... the Regional Board has been extremely concerned regarding aspects of your conduct ..." and (later in the letter) "we will not tolerate repetition of the conduct which led to it being referred to the Regional Board ...."

Please accurately describe what "conduct" that you, and the Regional Board, have expressed as being of concern.

Yours sincerely

Vic

REF 10 P3

The Broadway
Lancing
West Sussex BN15

5 October 2006

Mr V A Parks
1 Kiln Walk
Redhill
Surrey RH1 5SW

Dear Vic

Thank you for your letter dated 16 September 2006 in response to my letter dated 3 July 2006.

I circulated copies of your letter at last week's Regional Board meeting. The Regional Board expressed surprise that you are seeking clarification regarding aspects of the content of my letter, particularly as they are aware that prior to you being sent the letter, you were sent a copy of Karen Froggatt's paper to the Regional Board, in which she outlined her concerns regarding your conduct.

The Regional Board agreed that I should advise you that we consider the matter to be closed and that we will not be entering into further correspondence with you in this respect.

Yours sincerely

Adrienne Lowe
Regional Chair

14 news agenda   Co-operative Group Quinquennial Review

It's your choice ... a blueprint for the future? Or the final curtain for Co-op democracy?

CO-OPERATIVE GROUP activist VIC PARKS *(pictured)* discusses the issues which he believes should be at the heart of next year's Quinquennial Review and offers his own personal vision of the way ahead for the Group and the Movement

INSTEAD of being a measured and detailed analysis by the whole of the elected membership, the delayed Quinquennial Review is in danger of being a rushed and botched exercise.

In the wake of the postponement of the Review from 2004 until next year and the swingeing cuts imposed via Project Exchequer despite widespread opposition, there are serious concerns about the Co-operative Group's democratic structure.

Thus the review is a golden opportunity to strengthen co-operative democracy; make it work more effectively and ensure that elected members have real influence and control. In my view, the basic principle of member control being the unique and fundamental tenet of co-operative enterprise has been systematically undermined over the years. The Project

Exchequer cuts exacerbated this trend and in my experience, there is considerable frustration and anger that elected members are ignored, sidelined and made "impotent."

Ralph Taylor (formerly of the Sussex Area Committee) summed up the frustration of active members in January when he said in a letter to the *News* that the "democratic" processes of the Co-operative Group were "largely a façade".

Despite strong opposition and elected members' protestations, the Main Board implemented the Project Exchequer cuts.

Similar decisions (e.g. closure of non-food stores, food superstores, sale of Priory Motors), which deeply affect many of our members, were also just delivered from above as a fait accompli.

"Consultation" is often just a sham and this powerlessness is perhaps one of the reasons why there is political apathy in the wider community. Radical change is needed to address these problems. So why not consult widely among members and customers on proposed closures and why not use referendums as part of the decision-making process by the wider membership?

This would have the effect of making decision-making "bottom up" rather than "top down".

Assets

After all, when members' assets are being disposed of, or a service to them is being withdrawn, should they not have a say?

At the very least, decision making on fundamental issues with far reaching consequences ought to be taken region-wide using referendums among area committee members. Where possible, it ought to be

extended to ordinary members – the owners of our society.

And should not decisions of the regional boards be open to challenge within six weeks of decisions being distributed in the minutes?

Perhaps there could be a system of ratification, or not, by the next area committee meeting? This might help to address the frustration and powerlessness area committee members feel when decisions are handed down from above.

Principles

Key principles of democracy are freedom of speech and the right to free and open discussion. Debate on all sides of an issue is paramount.

One of my deep concerns is the lack of real debate of issues and policies. Over the years, the opportunities for discussion, sharing experience, expertise, views, and so on have been gradually eroded away.

For example, there are fewer opportunities to attend conferences, training workshops, summer schools, area committee conferences and so on.

Co-op events are often 'stand and deliver' in format, based upon the 'filling empty vessels [with knowledge]' training style. The 'platform' usually sits above the 'audience' who are often seated in rows.

Questioning is invariably formal, ie Stimulus - Response style with no right of "follow up" questions or questioning the reply. If one attempts this, he/she is accused of "heckling" and not of the "co-operative way".

So there needs to be more real debate by elected members; more opportunities for

Democracy debate must be heard

THE issue of confidentiality is especially pertinent to the situation elected representatives are in. Given that debate is essential between co-operators for effective democracy, the blanket use of 'confidentiality' could stifle any debate.

Committee members need to be clear as to what can and cannot be discussed outside the committee forum.

Identifying guidelines is difficult, but I would suggest there needs to be a list of specific instances, which are absolutely confidential (e.g. store closures, disciplining

of staff, etc.). Yet issues that relate to the democratic structure and processes ought to be open and transparent.

The test would be whether any breach would be of commercial advantage to a competitor.

I believe members should be protected by a 'whistle blowing' rule (ie: disclosure in the public, co-operative interest) in the same way as staff are protected.

Given that one of our basic co-op principles is openness, it must be ensured that discussion is facilitated, not suppressed.

REF 11 P2   25 JULY 2006   B4 to A4

THE WAY AHEAD ... Vic Parks believes the review should empower members so they have a say in major decisions, such as the sell-off of Priory Motors (above)

area committee members to meet region-wide and with others in other parts of the country.

Perhaps more "special, informal" area committee meetings, in addition to the normal "business," meetings are necessary.

The debate by members needs to be facilitated in a non-judgemental, open and friendly way. Offering more opportunities for face-to-face discussion is useless if it is contrived and controlled in an autocratic way.

In the past year, my area committee had two opportunities to adopt a much more informal, friendly and interactive mode of discussion using facilitators and circles of chairs.

The committee had a 'blue sky' meeting and the ordinary member's half-yearly meeting afternoon session was an open forum discussion.

Although 'open' questions were asked by the lead facilitator, the 'agenda' was set by the participants raising issues individually. Based on evaluation questionnaires, both forums were seen as being very successful.

The key difference is that peoples' concerns are written down, recorded and agreed, even if in a 'minority report'. Thus, there is a record to be acted upon and progress monitored.

Members

I would also like to see *Co-operative News* distributed more widely to members, customers and staff as a this would give everyone a better understanding of the issues that affect their society.

Reading the debate on fundamental issues and awareness of other independent co-operatives' good practice, ideas and innovation contributes to a vibrant Movement.

In addition, a computer debating forum needs to be properly established. This is particularly important for regional issues.

There is little doubt that there are concerns about the Co-operative Group, particularly in terms of its democracy, selling assets, education, training and management style.

How and in what depth the Quinquennial Review will address these issues and bring about meaningful reform is in the hands of the elected members. My fear is the 'Top Table' (through its Quinquennial Review Working Party) will filter proposals and suggestions.

It may simply tinker at the fringes (e.g. size of committees, numbers of regions, numbers of Board members and so on) without truly addressing the deep feelings of frustration and impotence many feel.

The issue is, has the Co-operative Group's servants become its masters? If so, the Quinquennial Review should fundamentally redress this imbalance.

When the documents appear, it is important that members are not presented with a "vote for it all, or reject it entirely" scenario.

Concept

Votes need to be taken proposal by proposal, preferably with options. As to the costs of my proposals, it has to be recognised that effective democracy costs money.

If the concept of co-operation is seen as a desirable goal, the costs must be seen as an investment for the future rather than a "drain on resources".

Being part of a £9 billion organisation, these are miniscule. As one of the largest co-operatives in the world, the Co-op Group is a flagship for the sector. As such, it is vital that it presents a model that all can respect and admire.

It is in the hands of the membership, at all levels, to address the perceived ills and to ensure that our organisation is deeply embedded within our co-operative principles and values, especially the democratic principle that emphasises the difference between co-operatives and PLCs.

• *Vic Parks is chair of the Co-operative Group's Surrey and Berkshire Area Committee, but writes in a personal capacity.*

What do you think?

DO you have a view on what issues should be addressed by the Co-op Group's forthcoming Quinquennial Review and how the process should work? Is Vic Parks correct in his belief that this is 'make or break' review which will shape the Group's future for generations to come – perhaps even forever?

If you would like to reply to any of the points made in these pages or air your own opinions, send your comments to: News Views, Co-operative News, Holyoake House, Hanover Street, Manchester M60 0AS or email them to: editorial@thenews.coop

FOUR ISSUES OF CONCERN

DEMOCRATIC STRUCTURE AND ROLES

• ALL members of the Main Board, including the representatives of the corporate membership, ought to be lay directors elected by the membership in my view. Currently, almost all the representatives of the corporates are Chief Officers/Executives. This could give rise to a bias in favour of the "Executive". In view of the widespread perception that the Executive has too much power, the present situation mitigates against the principle of democratic control by membership through its elected members.

• Area Committee size should reflect the number of trading outlets, geographical size, level/type of membership activities undertaken and financial turnover.

• Senior staff ought to be appointed from the ranks of co-operators. The shop floor to senior management ought to be the norm, rather than the exception. Their co-operative credentials must be clearly evident.

ROLE OF THE EXECUTIVE

• THERE is a widespread feeling the Executive is firmly in control. How many examples of suggestions being taken up can be identified as coming from an "ordinary" committee member? Active members often believe they are wasting their time and question the point of their involvement and commitment.

• The elected representatives should take strategic decisions in an informed way, with input from management, not be little more than "nodding donkeys".

• There needs to be a clear definition of roles and boundaries – the Executive providing information and guidance, but not strongly influencing outcomes. Members on committees are sometimes accused of sleep walking while important decisions are nodded through without proper debate or analysis. Often, this is due to shortage of time and crowded agendas. Some members do not want to "rock the boat", or do not fully appreciate the consequences of certain policies and proposals. The fundamental role of members is to hold the Executive to account.

STAFF AND MEMBERS RELATIONSHIP

• WHEN members of staff and elected members are in an intimate relationship, conflicts of interest may arise. A review is necessary to look at this issue.

THE AGE RULE

• THIS should be scrapped as it is fundamentally discriminatory and can deprive committees of talent and experience. The competence of members ought to be evaluated individually (e.g. some form of appraisal).

www.thenews.coop

22 ... views

'Negative' views are not representative of South East region

AT a recent meeting of the Co-operative Group South East Regional Board, members noted with concern, and indeed some alarm, the article by Vic Parks in the *Co-operative News* (July 25th) and the prominence given to his highly personal views.

Vic presents a negative and potentially demoralising account of what we believe will be a 'root and branch' review of the Group's democratic structures and practices, and of a review process that has already entailed widespread consultation and will doubtless entail much more discussion, analysis and consultation in coming months.

Constructive

The democratically elected regional board asked that I should write to the *News* in my capacity as regional chair, to indicate that we do not believe that Vic's views are representative of the 76 elected members within our region.

Also, we as a board certainly do not consider ourselves to be 'powerless', or that 'consultation is often just a sham'.

We in the South East region pride ourselves on being challenging, yet constructive, and we hope and believe this would be the view of other elected members across the country.

Our submission in the first stage of the consultation process was both wide-ranging and extensive.

It incorporated feedback from all elected bodies within the region, on the grounds that although we have a representative democratic structure, we value the input of our elected members at all levels. The constitutional review is most welcome and undoubtedly needs to tackle some fundamental issues.

It has only just begun and has many months to run. In a society the size of the Co-operative Group this is both necessary and appropriate.

We need to ensure that we get it right, and that we have practices which are fit for purpose in today's fast moving retail environment, yet which reflect our distinct ownership model.

The regional board believes that this is achievable, particularly if we are all working to the same objective.

A small point of accuracy, contrary to what is said in the article, Vic is no longer Chair of Surrey & Berkshire Area Committee.

ADRIENNE LOWE
CHAIR, CO-OPERATIVE GROUP
SOUTH EAST REGIONAL BOARD

EDITOR'S NOTE: The reference to Vic Parks being the current chair of the Co-operative Group's Surrey & Berkshire Area Committee was a production error by the News. Mr Parks has now stepped down from this position. Our apologies for any inconvenience caused.

Co-ops need to embrace trend

CO-OP WEB ... The uk.coop site is the focal point of all things co-operative in the UK

MAT COWARD'S letter (August 8th) raises an important point about the promotion of co-operative values and principles and how we as a Movement can increase the level of understanding and awareness, especially among younger people.

I agree absolutely with Mat's statement that co-operative ideas are more strongly in tune with the views of many people today than they have been for many years, and it is our responsibility as a Movement to capitalise on that.

At Co-operatives UK we seek to help our member organisations promote understanding of co-operation and in particular to raise awareness of what makes co-operatives 'different'.

Much of this work is carried out through diverse means ranging from the development of our social and co-operative performance indicators through the development of the online directory of UK co-operatives at www.uk.coop to the training provided by the Co-operative College (of which Co-operatives UK is the trustee).

We also recognise that as well as working with our co-operative members, we also have a role in communicating directly to the general public about the Co-operative Movement, and our website is ou primary means of doing this.

It is with this role firmly in mind that we are currently in the process of redesigning our website – with one of our key objectives being to present clear, simple and concise information that answers the question: "What is a co-operative?"

We will of course be very pleased to work with any and all of our members (or indeed any of the 2650+ co-operative organisations in the UK) to make this information available for their use – they may even wish to disseminate it in the form of a leaflet for their stores, etc., if they so choose.

GRAHAM MITCHEL
MARKETING & COMMUNICATIONS OFFICE
CO-OPERATIVES U

Brown deserves to lose his seat

THE Co-op News editorial (July 25th) was very interesting. It is true that the Gordon Brown has indicated his support for nuclear weapons of mass destruction.

Gordon Brown must surely think that the problem of poverty has been solved if he is going to agree to the wasting of £27/£28 billion on the upgrading of the Trident nuclear weapons system.

Gordon Brown, in my opinion, deserves to lose his parliamentary seat never mind the matter of replacing that other warmonger, Tony Blair.

Your editorial suggests that Gordon Brown has "acquiesed" on the matter of Iraq. In fact, sadly, Gordon Brown writes the multi-billion pound war cheques on behalf of the Labour Government.

No wonder "the Chancellor's succession looks a lot less assured".

ALASDAIR RUSSELL
PAISLEY

Due to a production error, Mike Paxton's letter (August 8th) should have read "between the earth's seven and six billion population", not 76 billion. Our apologies for any confusion caused.

READERS' letters must be addressed to the editor, signed and accompanied by the full address (not necessarily for publication). *Co-operative News* reserves the right to edit letters.

Send your letters to:
Postbag, Co-operative News, Holyoake House, Hanover Street, Manchester M60 0AS.

You can also respond direct to an article immediately at www.thenews.coop

E-mail: editorial@thenews.coop   Fax: 0161 214 0878

www.thenews.coop

We can make history

IT is pleasing to know that a recent Mori poll found that more people are interested in history than in football.

Clearly the time is ripe for the co-operative, Labour and trade union movements to take a prominent part in the campaign to create more awareness of our national heritage and the country's international role.

Let us try to ensure the history of the 'British way of life' to the presen day records the salient role of the Labour Movement in all its aspects.

BILL JORD/
DEV(

REF 13   5 – 19 SEPT 2006

stake to link key issues

...tor of Brand Development ...hat a national member- ...confirms what I have deter- ...er the last few months. ...he Co-operative Group ...societies are read by the ...d by point of sale systems ...That is the card that is ...as a Co-op membership ...be done with the informa- ...ably nothing. ...nnology for a common ...y soon be in place is also ...t several societies and ...ake a new issue of cards ...r availability". ...to the era of dividend ...sition where local recipro- ...d. ...petition restrictions may ...ore than one society to ...society's dividend and ...of a given society's inde- ...hip base. ...plemented by a rule ...ore than £5 a year with a ...s not a member, then £1 ...ship granted. ...s than £1 in a year with

that society in later years the membership could automatically terminate and the pound be refunded along with any other dividends due. This would help keep all records up to date.

However it seems to me that it would be a retrograde step if the common membership system is going to be linked with the new brand project.

Many societies currently possess a far more valuable local brand image which they are going to find it impossible to ditch in favour of the new brand project except at great loss (and brands are valuable).

Distinction

Furthermore, the new brand for food stores makes no distinction between stores with different pricing. Currently in one area stores with a red cloverleaf have the most competitive prices, those with green intermediate prices and those with blue – the Co-operative Group convenience stores – are the most expensive of all.

Everybody at least is clear what is what. Linking the implementation of two possibly good ideas unnecessarily could and perhaps will cause one or both to fail on the demerits of the other which would be a crying shame.

HUGH BRIDGE
LONGFIELD, KENT

Free speech vital

I FEEL uneasy that the Chair of the South East Regional Board should write to the *News* to protest about comments made by Vic Parks (July 25th).

Mr Parks was clearly writing in a personal capacity and he, like many members, is unhappy with some of the current policies of the Co-op Group.

I have often made my views known in letters to the *News*, but where I disagree with Mr Parks is that I am happy that the SE Regional Board have addressed many of my concerns. While they may not always have the power or influence to change policies, they are aware of member concerns.

I have offered my views on the Group's democratic structure as a committee member and no doubt there will be much discussion in the future.

However, I am concerned that there appears to be a 'witch hunt' against some outspoken members (not me I hasten to add) and this should not happen in a democratic organisation. Why must criticism result in accusations that the critics are not working to the same objectives?

COLIN RICHELL
LONDON N13

New brand benefits all

IT is good news that Leeds Co-op is to start trialling the new The co-operative brand. Let's hope its the first of many announcements that regional societies are prepared to take part in this exciting project to the benefit of the entire Movement.

ANDREW HANTON
ABERDEEN

MSPs still focusing on mutual ideas

...Parliament election ...good time to reflect on ...ivered for Scotland. ...progress bringing real ...munities. Health waiting ...xam results are up, crime ...ber of people in work is up ...rty are down. Our senior ...after with free personal ...installed in their homes ...us travel.

built

...ear old now has access to ...nd we are now moving on ...for two year olds in our ...s. ...ndergoing the most radical ...tion, and we are tackling ...hat has made life a misery ...o long.

By Cathy Jamieson

overseas undergraduates, as well as those genuinely seeking refuge from persecution.

In the three years that our Fresh Talent policy has been in place, Scotland has seen the greatest net gain in migration since records began.

The Scottish Parliament has a strong Co-op Group of MSPs who have continued to shape

bring forward a micro-renewables Bill, similar to that promoted in Westminster by Mark Lazarowicz MP. Ideas for co-operative and mutual models for health and social care have been raised with Ministers.

As we move towards 2007, the Co-op Group of MSPs is again playing its part in developing thinking for the future as we face the challenges ahead considering, for example, how we might extend co-operative and mutual models in providing public services, whether we can extend the successful approach of Supporters Direct into other areas, and how can we further grow our credit unions and extend the range of services they provide.

Progress

Devolution has given us to the opportunity to face up to Scotland's problems and create Scottish solutions while working closely with our Westminster colleagues.

It's also given us the chance to set out own priorities of social justice and a fairer, safer country for all

REF 14

The Co-operative Group – South East Region

EXTRACT FROM MINUTES OF REGIONAL BOARD MEETING
HELD ON 28 JUNE 2007

Further to discussion at the previous meeting regarding Vic Parks' conduct, the Regional Secretary referred to legal advice she had received between meetings regarding the course of action proposed.

The Regional Board recalled the matters of concern most recently, ie:

- Vic Parks' conduct at the Group SGM, where he had disregarded the action agreed by the delegation at the pre-meeting, and where his conduct had led to the Regional Chair speaking to disassociate the Region from his comments
- his letter to Co-op News in April 2007, which it was felt had reflected negatively on the Regional Board and management. It was noted that due to pressures on the Regional Board agenda, action in this respect had been carried forward to the following meeting, at which Vic's conduct at the SGM was also considered.

The Regional Board stressed that it did not wish to restrict freedom of speech, though felt that it was essential that regional delegates should agree (and adhere to) a collective course of action, and that all delegates should conduct themselves in an appropriate manner.

Discussion took place regarding the way forward in respect of the ongoing concerns regarding Vic Parks' conduct. It was agreed that instead of initiating formal proceedings under the Code of Conduct, the Regional Board would ask Surrey & Berkshire Area Committee to note the Regional Board's concerns and to cease selecting Vic Parks as one of their delegates to any major conferences/events for a fixed period.

It was agreed that the Minute outlining the Regional Board's deliberations in this respect would be communicated to members of Surrey & Berkshire Area Committee, further to which the three Regional Board members on Surrey & Berkshire Area Committee would be able to convey the Regional Board's concerns to their colleagues on the Area Committee.

REF 15 P1

SPECIAL GENERAL MEETING 27 APRIL 2007, DELEGATE'S REPORT

BY VIC PARKS

As expected, the motion 6 to support the merger went through. You should have received the full results on each motion from Manchester. Only one region was opposed, the South West. Their representative, Peter Begley (former Group and CRS Director) gave a very cutting and pertinent formal speech which "pressed many buttons" for me. For example, why was it that we had the cuts under Project Exchequer yet there is money around for substantial rises in fees and compensatory payments? He pointed to the immorality of the merger taking place with the Peter Marks being guaranteed the top job as Chief Executive, as a condition of the merger. Why was there not a selection process? Why could not Martin Beaumont continue as Chief Executive? He pointed to past mergers where similar conditions had led to problems (i.e. failures).

Bob Burlton (Chair) stated that there would be a presentation and debate on the Business Case (by Martin Beaumont [CE] based on the document "Stronger Together") followed by the same by Nick Eyre for the constitutional changes (rules and constitutional Review Board). Formal voting on the motions would follow this.

I have to say that the whole delegation system is somewhat nonsensical. Delegations have already decided what they are going to vote so what is the point of the speeches and "debate" from the floor? I always thought the reason for "debate" of motions was to persuade the meeting of the arguments. The most democratic system I have witnessed is Co-op Party Annual Conference. The majority of our delegation at a 9 am meeting, before SGM simply went along with what was Minuted at the last delegates meeting after the Area Committee Conference (in your March meeting' papers).

My emails to our AC the week prior to the SGM appear to have been circulated to high levels, with Nick Eyre replying to them. It also appears, from the remark of Bob Harber, that they went around Regional Board. I raised the issue of the Independent Professional Non-elected Directors and it was agreed that I would speak on this. I again raised the issue about United changing its rules so that it could borrow up to ten times its assets. Four copies of United's accounts were placed on the table. Mike Hedgethorn stated that they had borrowed £210M. I am not an accountant, and we had no time to study the accounts. There was a reference to "Intangible Assets of, I think, £275M," whatever that means.

I raised both these issues at the SGM, proper. If nothing else, a benchmark had been registered. If at any time in the future a stone is turned over and a Black Hole appears, at least their attention had been drawn to the issue. I referred also to the Alldays and Balfours acquisitions, which drove us into financial trouble because the Board were not aware of the hidden liabilities that they had taken on. With regard to IPNEDS, Nick Eyre emphasised that the interim Board could **not** appoint them, only to CFS when a vacancy occurred. So, fears of an unlimited number being appointed to the Main Board were allayed. I also raised the issue of Nick Eyre having powers to use his sole discretion without reference back to the Main Board, which some of you expressed concern. Bob Burlton reassured the SGM that these would only be limited to altering punctuation, or rewording proving it did not alter the rule makers' intentions. I was content with this. However, I felt that it was important for this to be clarified. Finally, I raised the issue of ICL and the wasted costs. The Co-op News had reported costs of £5M, although Nick Eyre reported that both sides had agreed to stop the action, each paying their own costs – Groups being £2M, although I am not sure that included

REF 15 P2

the cost of the Appeal. In any event, the action was fruitless and cost at least £2M. He said that the original trial judge was mad.

CONSTITUTIONAL REVIEW BOARD

I know that greater democratic control is high on our AC's agenda. Since this was an opportunity to emphasise the issue, I started my address with a quote from Alan Middleton, past Congress President and part time lecturer for Co-operative College:

"The Movement is over dominated by paid officers....employees of the movement- who will not rest until the voice of the lay member has been completely silenced."

I emphasised that the grass roots voices want to be heard, with more democracy and decision making to the grass roots, mentioning the principle of one member one vote. I expressed concern that the Review Board was made up entirely of Top Table and that there ought to be more grass roots representation and that "consultation" ought to be "meaningful." I did get a ripple of applause at the end, but probably, the majority of the meeting were directors rather than grass roots members.

In reply Steve Watts (Board Deputy Chair) stated that it was up to you (grassroots) to pass the new rules and that he could not get things past us that we did not want (of course, it depends upon the way they are presented and the time we have to properly evaluate them. Has not our experience been limited time and everything in a rush?) He did say that devolving power down to Regions was an issue and the wish to engage the membership. This being fraught, he said, with the problem of involving them more, but then blocking them due to lack of space on Area Committees.

A question on Members Councils, that United have (like Member Relations Committees) and whether these would remain. This was also in the melting pot. (We have discussed the possibilities of meeting local customers in joint sessions, if my memory is correct.)

Other issues:

United provide copies of Co-op News at all retail outlets. Concern by the Press Board was expressed whether these should be maintained. (In the past, I have advocated this for Group, perhaps given out when the customer's shopping exceeds a certain amount). It was confirmed that this issue would be addressed as part of the Constitutional review. In the interim, there would be no change to the arrangement for either the Group or United stores. A view from the floor was that the Co-op News should be maintained to previous Committee members.

The independent societies have had reassurance that they would not be coerced into joining Group and that current buying arrangements would be maintained.

The most contentious issue was the compensatory payments, as this might set a precedent and influence directors to make future mergers. Adrienne Lowe stated that the SE had swallowed this "bitter pill" of compensation payments to ensure that the merger went ahead.

I had made it clear that the views I expressed were mine and I was raising some issues raised by my Area Committee and not the SE delegation's.

Vic Parks

1 May 2007

Group should seek the views of its entire membership

REF 16 CO-OP NEWS 10 JUNE 2008

Letters

Letters must be addressed to the editor and accompanied by the full address (not necessarily for publication). Co-operative News reserves the right to edit letters. Send letters to: Postbag, Co-operative News, Holyoake House, Hanover Street, Manchester, M60 0AS. Email: editorial@thenews.coop or fax: 0161 214 0878.

AT the outset of the Constitutional Review, I predicted that it would change little other than perhaps the discriminatory Age Rule and tinker with some structures. This appears to be the case and with the "top table" firmly in control of the process, it was to be expected.

The Review has not addressed the fundamental problems besetting the Group's democracy, the principle of "owned and controlled by its members".

Throughout the Review there has been the unchallenged assumption that the Group should be a representative democracy. The debate has centred on the form it should take. Direct democracy through referenda has not even been considered in the "consultation documents".

As many who have sat through years of "consultation" know, there is often a fixed agenda with the outcomes largely predetermined. Few (if any) consultation documents are binned or radically altered after the "consultation process".

The Review Committee will point to the road shows and lay committee consultation to justify the legitimacy of the report's recommendations. What I witnessed at the road show was the usual sham, a process whereby the meeting asks questions and makes comments and the platform responds with no proper debate.

It is a sterile, controlled exercise where those who control the agenda can accept or reject views in private without scrutiny, transparency or explanation. With predetermined outcomes (i.e. maintenance of the Group's current democratic structure) they can "legitimise" their decisions in the Constitutional Review pamphlet.

That falls far short of a reflective, analytical report showing how the committee arrived at its decisions, other than occasional cursory explanations.

Transparency

As to lower tier consultation (area committees), that is funnelled through regional boards again without transparency or explanation. Thus, a small group of perhaps 15 people with their own personal agendas and prejudices decide a region's view purporting to represent up to around 500,000 members.

After roughly three years (including the Quinquennial Review) and much grass roots huffing and puffing, the Group's status quo is maintained, albeit with a bit of tinkering.

The size of the main/regional boards, area committees, independent non-executive directors is little more than a diversion from the core tenet of ownership and control by the members. As it stands, the real power remains in the hands of a few lay individuals, the management and secretariat.

In one of the consultation documents the test of governance was that "members must vote for the structure". But, under present arrangements, it will be just a 100 or so who will have that right, claiming to represent the 3,000,000 ordinary members.

It is hypocritical for the Group to apparently champion the increase in membership yet curbs its fundamental democratic rights, so I challenge the Main Board to hold a referendum of the whole active membership to decide the route for their co-operative.

Clearly, there would be a need to lay out proposals identifying the detailed arguments for one-member-one-vote meetings and/or referenda versus the current representative democracy. The use of an independent balloting organisation (e.g. the Electoral Reform Society) would ensure that the arguments on both sides are put objectively with a valid vote.

VIC PARKS
SURREY
(vic.parks@ntlworld.com)

Are directors protecting their

Don't discard

www.ingramcontent.com/pod-product-compliance
Lightning Source LLC
Chambersburg PA
CBHW080304180526
45167CB00006B/2662